The Prodigal's Wilderness:

WHEN THE "WRONG" PATH
REALLY IS THE RIGHT PATH

by

Sue White

Published by Best Seller Publishing®, Pasadena, CA
Best Seller Publishing® is a registered trademark
Printed in the United States of America.

This publication is designed to provide accurate and authoritative information with regard to the subject matter covered. It is sold with the understanding that the publisher is not engaged in rendering legal, accounting, or other professional advice. If legal advice or other expert assistance is required, the services of a competent professional should be sought. The opinions expressed by the authors in this book are not endorsed by Best Seller Publishing® and are the sole responsibility of the author rendering the opinion.

Most Best Seller Publishing® titles are available at special quantity discounts for bulk purchases for sales promotions, premiums, fundraising, and educational use. Special versions or book excerpts can also be created to fit specific needs.

For more information, please write:
Best Seller Publishing®
1346 Walnut Street, #205
Pasadena, CA 91106
or call 1(626) 765 9750
Toll Free: 1(844) 850-3500
Visit us online at: www.BestSellerPublishing.org

TABLE OF CONTENTS

TABLE OF CONTENTS

The test of a first-rate intelligence is the ability to hold two opposed ideas in mind at the same time and still retain the ability to function.

F. Scott Fitzgerald

PREFACE

A Parable of Transformation

Much has been written regarding Luke Chapter 15 and there's been a great debate regarding which theme(s) should be considered and which one(s) ignored; however, this book will take a different approach by viewing it as a parable of transformation.

Jesus used a unique storytelling technique in this parable: the main characters changed and grew. They transformed from their initial negative personas (they had all either lost something valuable, or they themselves were "lost") to the positive persona of the seeker, the one who found and restored the lost object. In so doing, they came to represent both God and Jesus.

As we explore the transformations of the main characters, we will derive principles that can be applied to our own lives and our own wilderness experiences.

The Transformations Happened in the Wilderness

The wilderness (or desert) is the place where transformations occur. As you read through the Bible, you'll see that God had many of the heroes of the faith participate in their own wilderness adventures, for example: Moses and the Israelites, David, Elijah, John the Baptist and even Jesus. They were all transformed by their desert experiences.

It may seem that time spent in the desert is wasted time, but in reality, the solitude and isolation of the desert allow God to accelerate our spiritual growth and increase intimacy with him. He wants to develop a "real," in-depth relationship with us and he will use whatever means necessary to make that happen. For example, he often uses family or political conflict, natural or economic disasters, health conditions, or loss of a significant person in our lives to drive us to our knees and put him first in our lives.

The desert is God's preferred learning laboratory for believers. All believers will likely spend some time in the wilderness, in God's "boot camp." Some will enroll multiple times. But, the bottom line is this: God is still in control and he has a plan to conform you to his image (Rom. 12:2) so that he can have greater fellowship. God is sovereign even when you're in the midst of a wilderness experience and feeling scared, confused or overwhelmed.

The wilderness may seem like it's the "wrong" path, that you've gotten lost or strayed from God, but he can redeem even the most crooked path and use all of your experiences along the way for good (Rom. 8:28).

The "Right" Path May Contain Detours and U-Turns

The two sons in the third story demonstrate that there are basically two paths that you can take in life – a path that takes you closer to God, or one that takes you away from him. Sometimes, the right path can be circuitous. It may appear that you are on the wrong path, when in reality it is just God's plan for you to spend time being molded and refined into the person you were created to be.

In the end, the "right" path ultimately brings you closer to God whereas the wrong path ultimately takes you further away from him. You can't really tell until you get to the end of the path. People in your life may be critical of your life choices, but in reality, they may not be seeing God's hand at work in your life, invisibly, behind the scenes. Consequently, you need to be true to yourself and trust God to bring you home, and he will!

God created us in his image; complex human beings comprised of biological, psychological, and spiritual components. We're also deeply influenced by our families and our culture. He wants to enter into a real relationship with us, one that includes all our human complexity. He understands the inter-relationship between psychology and spirituality and how the past affects our present (after all, he created us). He understands how emotional baggage carried over from childhood can impact your relationship with him. He understands a lot of the sinful nature still needs to be stripped away. When he redeems us, he redeems all of us, the whole package, and he makes us into new creatures (II Cor. 5:17). In other words, he transforms us.

A Personal Note

This book is based on a paper I wrote when I was in grad school, but a lot has transpired in my life since I wrote that paper. It's been a difficult journey for me – one filled with lots of health challenges, multiple job changes, and several relocations. But the experiences I had while on my journey and my own personal "wilderness experiences" have taught me many important life lessons.

I have always been the studious type, a "bookworm;" I'm a lifelong learner, and I have an eclectic background. Over the years, I have acquired four earned degrees including a Masters in Theological Studies and a Masters in Marriage and Family Therapy. I studied psychology because I like to figure out "what makes people tick". (I had planned to become a psychotherapist - until a serious illness derailed that plan.)

I relate to the skeptics of the world – those who need to ask questions and challenge the status quo in order to find the truth. (My favorite disciple is Thomas, otherwise known as "Doubting Thomas"). I remember, as a child, asking questions in Sunday school, but seldom receiving answers that satisfied me. Eventually, God sent me to seminary so that I could learn to search out Scriptural answers for myself.

I currently lead a small group Bible Study for people in my neighborhood. My background allows me to draw insights from multiple disciplines and to integrate them into a cohesive whole. I'm the kind of person who sees patterns and looks for the "big picture". I take a holistic view and try to put all the pieces together into a coherent whole.

When I'm teaching, I love having people ask lots of questions. I find that people learn best when they're engaged and asking questions increases engagement. I especially welcome the skeptic (the one who is honestly searching but just not convinced) to join in wholeheartedly with the discussions.

As you read through the book, ask yourself questions. Interact with the material. Get engaged with the message. You will get a lot more out of this study if you challenge the parable – and me – as you read.

Background to Writing This Book

My own life's path has been a circuitous one; in fact, one of my friends used to call it "peripatetic" since, as a consultant, I traveled from place to place for my work. Mine was quite a different lifestyle from the rest of my family who stayed in the area where we grew up.

The idea for this book was born about twenty-five years ago, while I was in seminary. I had to write a paper for one of my classes. Normally, when I'd write a paper in college, I would struggle with it until it was complete, turn it in, get my grade, and move on. *However, this paper was different - there was something special about it.* (But, like all my other college papers, I simply filed it away and forgot about it.)

After grad school, I worked as a consultant for many years, and I moved around a lot. It seemed that every time I moved, I "downsized" just a little bit more – but, you know what? That paper always seemed to find its way into one of my moving boxes. (The rest of my college papers have long since fallen by the wayside). Recently, this paper *"called out to me,"* wanting to become a book and get published.

I had begun the study for my paper – like so many people before me – by looking at the "Parable of the Prodigal Son" as a standalone parable. However, I quickly realized that doing so was a "red herring". I was shocked to discover the number of differing views and interpretations provided – and the number of assumptions commentators made in developing their interpretations. Most of their interpretations seemed merely to confirm the author's preconceived ideas.

I quickly realized that single story wasn't the complete parable, and it didn't fully answer the Pharisees' criticism of Jesus' eating with sinners. I understood that the parable had to include all three stories in Luke Chapter 15, not just the third story. As I studied this material, I became more and more impressed with its depth and beauty. I hope that you will discover that depth and beauty as you read this book, and that it will encourage you to dig even deeper into this parable on your own.

Who Should Read This Book? Everyone!

This book is intended for everyone: for seekers, skeptics, "prodigals", and long-time Christians. The parable addresses universal questions such as *"Who am I?"* and *"What should I do with my life?"* It addresses universal needs of love, acceptance, intimacy, recognition, and self-worth. It demonstrates that you need God to come find you and save you because you can't save yourself; it explains that you have a loving Father and a home waiting for you in heaven.

Feel Like You're in the Wilderness Right Now?

Are you feeling sort of lost and overwhelmed in your life right now? Don't know which way to turn? Perhaps you've just lost your job, or been hit with the dreaded "C" diagnosis from your doctor. Perhaps you just have too much month left over at the end of your money. Maybe you've lost a loved one and you're feeling lonely and depressed.

Maybe God has just signed you up for one of his wilderness courses. They're usually not very much fun, and may actually include a fair amount of pain and suffering, but they do have a number of important benefits, not the least of which is developing a closer relationship with God. *Just have faith, and stay the course – God will get you through!* (He's there with you, every day and every step of the way on your wilderness journey even though it probably doesn't feel like he is right now. And above, don't think he's angry with you!) All believers, at one time or another, have the "privilege" of taking one of God's wilderness courses!

Think God Is Angry With You?

Do you ever feel like God is silent, so therefore, he must be angry with you? This book is meant to serve as an encouragement to those of you who feel far from God. *Be encouraged – he loves you!* Sometimes, periods of silence, or suffering, or struggle (what I'm calling the "wilderness experience") are necessary for your growth and to build your faith.

After all, if you can constantly "see" what God is doing in your lives, and the world around you, you would have no need for faith, but the Bible tells you that faith is a necessity: *"Now faith is the substance of things hoped for, the evidence of things not seen"* (Heb. 11:1 KJV).

Feel Criticized, Rejected, Ostracized?

Some of you may identify with the prodigal son in the third story… you may feel that you've been criticized, rejected and ostracized by your family or friends. You may wonder if there's any possible way for you to regain fellowship with your family or friends. But, know this – there is hope for you! This parable speaks volumes about separation, reconciliation, and restoration. *Stay tuned! God loves you!*

Intimidated by God?

Some of you may have trouble relating to the seemingly judgmental, warrior God of the Old Testament; if so, you may find that you relate better to the God described in this parable, one who is more loving and compassionate (even feminine). Maybe you've been taught that you need to fear God, and you've spent your life running from him, but you didn't know that God loves you and wants what's best for your life. Now, you can *relax and stop running*. Discover the "hound of heaven," who is actively seeking to bring you into an intimate relationship with him.

Parent of a Wayward Child?

Others of you may have a son or daughter who has taken a lifestyle direction that you don't understand, or appreciate. You may even consider that child to be a "prodigal". There is hope for you (and for your child) in this parable. God can redeem all of your life choices. *Relax. God is in control!*

Benefits of Reading This Book

You may be wondering why you should read this book. How will you benefit? You can benefit from this material in a number of ways: it will introduce you to Jesus the Messiah, help strengthen your Christian walk, and improve your ministry to your friends, neighbors, community … maybe even, the world!

Here's a quick overview of some of the benefits you can expect by reading this book.

Meet the Messiah!

If you've never met Jesus, the Messiah, now's your chance! Be sure to pay attention to the Chapter, *"Who Is This Jesus?"* You'll learn about the man, his mission, his ministry – and the changes he brought that have impacted the world for two thousand years!

Improve Your Personal Bible Study

Some of you just love to study Scripture and discover new Biblical truths. I've packed a lot of Bible knowledge into the pages that follow. You will find much of the information about the culture and norms of first century Israel very fascinating. You may find that studying this parable helps you deepen your own Bible study methods and personal devotions. Some of those little historical tidbits may open your eyes to important Biblical truths you'd never seen before.

Become a More Critical Thinker

As Christians, you have an increasing need – and an increasing responsibility - to become critical thinkers; not just for your own benefit but also to benefit your families, your communities and the world around you. The Bible reminds you that you should expect to encounter false teachers, even more so, in the latter days:

> But there were also false prophets among the people, just as there will be false teachers among you. They will secretly introduce destructive heresies, even denying the sovereign Lord who bought them—bringing swift destruction on themselves.[2] Many will follow their depraved conduct and will bring the way of truth into disrepute.[3] In their greed these teachers will exploit you with fabricated stories" (II Peter 2:1-2a).

Be Prepared to Give An Answer

In today's post-Christian world, Christians are increasingly under attack for traditional Biblical beliefs. The devil and his minions are becoming much more active and much more vocal than they have been in the past. People from many walks of life, whether they be entertainers and celebrities, or politicians and protesters, or your next door neighbor, seem to take great pleasure in denigrating the Christian faith and your beliefs.

But there are moments, like the sun breaking through the clouds, when someone you know might actually be open to hearing the gospel and why you believe what you believe,

Always be prepared to give an answer to everyone who asks you to give the reason for the hope that you have. But do this with gentleness and respect. (I Peter 3:15)

Yours may be the only lucid voice they will ever hear that can introduce them to the Savior. Don't let such an opportunity pass you by because you were not prepared.

One of my favorite movies is "*God Is Not Dead*" (the first one). A young man in college finds himself stuck in a philosophy course with a very anti-God professor, and God calls him to take a personal stand and defend the proposition "God is not dead" to the class. This young man had to stand alone, facing criticism, opposition, rejection from his friends, and the threat of failing the class from his professor. But, by standing up for his faith, and presenting a cogent argument for the existence of the living God, he influenced a lot of other students who would never have heard about the God who loves them.

Like the young man in the movie, God may call some of you to carry out a difficult and unpopular task. You may find your life's path takes you to places you would never have dreamed, and you will have to rely upon God's strength and wisdom because the challenge is far greater than your human abilities. You all need the kind of fortitude demonstrated by the young man in the movie.

I trust that all of you will gain a greater appreciation for the depth and wisdom of this parable, and that reading this book will bless you and your family.

INTRODUCTION

God Loves Wildernesses

God seems to love wildernesses and deserts; they have a way of getting our undivided attention, providing a sacred space for spiritual transformation, and drawing us closer to him. Wilderness experiences seem to be God's preferred method for accelerating spiritual growth and development – or for providing positive divine discipline. Sometimes important life lessons can only be learned in God's crucible; they can only be learned through first-person experience, not from books or movies or another person.

Two Basic Types of Wildernesses

There are two basic types of wilderness experiences that God uses. I refer to the first one as the *"Wilderness Testing Challenge"* and I call the second one the *"Wilderness Communication Intensive."*

Wilderness Testing Challenge

In the *"Wilderness Testing Challenge,"* God has some tests in store for you; *the assumption being that you will pass!* But, in the meantime, you'll struggle; the tests and challenges are difficult, stressful and sometimes, they can feel overwhelming. There may be health challenges, financial challenges, family conflicts, a crisis of faith, or any other type of "disruptive change" event.

Disruptive changes are called "disruptive" for a good reason – they totally disrupt your normal, day-to-day life. They turn your daily routines and assumptions about how life works upside down. They confuse, distress, and overpower you as they announce a whole new order (think the wheel, the light bulb, 9/11, or the loss of a loved one). This is true regardless whether the change itself is positive one, or negative.

God's overall goal for this wilderness experience; however, is a positive one. He wants you to develop an intimate relationship with him and come to depend upon him fully. He wants to accelerate your spiritual growth and bring you closer to maturity. He wants you to learn to trust him and obey him, but to do so out of love rather than duty or obligation, and he certainly won't force you to love him. He respects your free will far too much to do that.

Wilderness Communication Intensive

In the "*Wilderness Communication Intensive*," God wants you to draw closer to him and develop a deep covenantal relationship with him. The objective is to provide an environment free of the normal day-to-day distractions so that you can hear his "still, small voice" as he speaks to you. You'll need plenty of undisturbed "quality" time to get to know God better and commune with him on a one-to-one basis. He may want to visit areas of prayer, worship, priorities, and possibly even personal sacrifice. God wants to develop a real relationship with you, one that is intimate, trusting and satisfies your needs for belonging, significance and security.

Goals of the Wilderness

God Is Transforming You

If you are in a wilderness today, be glad, because God is transforming you (II Cor. 5:17). Your goal should **not be** to escape from the desert, but rather, to learn whatever lessons God has for you, and then move on.

The desert is not a place to put down roots or stay for a long time. The environment is too harsh for long-term sustainability and happiness. You are only passing through; you don't want to live there.

God Uses the Desert to Prepare You

God uses the desert to prepare you, mold you, and build your character (Eph. 2:10). Sometimes, this preparation can happen quickly, but other times it may take a long time (with John the Baptist, it took 30 years, but then he had a critically important ministry to prepare for!). God's goal is to strip away all the "chaff" of life, refine you and reveal your true self; the person he created you to be. (Michelangelo once said, *"I saw the angel in the marble and carved until I set him free."*)

God Wants to Develop an Intimate Relationship with You

God wants you to get to know him as he really is, not how you may have been taught since childhood. He wants to reveal himself to you in ways that meet your needs and speak to your true self. He wants you to love him because of who he is, not because of the "toys" he gives you. He wants you to create a secure attachment to him, to love and worship him, and to find joy in your relationship with him. He wants to bring you to a position where you give up self-reliance and learn to depend upon him alone. He wants you to be able to rest in his presence and enjoy his fellowship.

Wilderness Requires You to Stretch Your Faith

The wilderness experience will almost always require you to stretch your faith. You probably won't be able to see God's purpose or his end result (until it's over), and that makes it stressful for you, but God has a plan for your spiritual development. He has everything under control (despite how things may appear), and you need to develop sufficient faith to believe in his sovereignty, even in the desert.

The Parable of Transformation

The parable in Luke 15 is one of Jesus' more complex parables – there's a lot happening. This parable encompasses multiple stories, characters, settings, themes as well as many psychological and theological issues. This book will focus on the transformations the characters undergo, as well as the psychological and theological processes that are involved in those transformations.

Jesus used a very interesting technique: the characters grow and develop; they "morph." In particular, he used the same character at the beginning of the story to represent negative traits to be avoided, and then later, he used that same character to represent positive traits and behaviors he wanted his audience to emulate.

As you review the person of Jesus, his public ministry, and especially his use of the parabolic genre, you will discover how his mission related directly to his message and his extensive use of parables. As Marshall McLuhan has said, *"The medium is the message."* We will explore the commonalities of the three stories and discover what they have to tell us about wildernesses and the transformations that occur therein.

CHAPTER 1

HISTORICAL OVERVIEW OF ISRAEL

Understanding the historical-cultural background of the Jewish people is a necessary first step in grasping the depth of this parable. To get a better sense of what Jesus' audience would have known and understood, we will look at ancient Israel for a broad sweep of major historical events.

Israel, as used in this book, refers to the ancient Jews living during the first century A.D. in the geographic area encompassing modern-day Israel, Palestine, Lebanon, Jordan and Syria. Some people use the term "Palestine" to refer to the land of the Jews during first century, but that is a pejorative term coined by the Romans, and it is inaccurate (it did not include all of the Holy Land). Jesus and Matthew used the term "Israel" even though the Romans did not, and the Bible never used the term "Palestine" to refer to the Holy Land as a whole. Recently some Arabs have adopted this term and they use it in an anti-Israeli manner.

To avoid any political overtones associated with the name "Palestine," I will refer to the land as either Israel or Judea.

We will consider the social, political, historical, religious and cultural situations as they impact this parable, as well as commonly understood symbols and their spiritual referents. We will evaluate Luke's background and that of his gospel. We will also review Jesus' mission to understand what his intentions may have been.

An overriding characteristic of the Jewish people is their belief in God (Yahweh) and the Hebrew Scriptures, so we'll start there.

Religious Background

Covenants formed the basis of the relationship between God and his people. They included promises given under oath and were legally binding; they were judicial in nature. There were six separate covenants with promises:

1) The Noahic Covenant (Gen. 6:18; 9:8–17),
2) The Abrahamic Covenant (Gen. 15:1–21, 17:1–22, 26:2–5:24),
3) *The Mosaic (Old) Covenant* (Ex. 19–20, 24),
4) The Priestly Covenant (Num. 25:10–13),
5) The Davidic Covenant (2 Sam. 7:12–16), and
6) *The New Covenant* (Jer. 31:31–34)

Only the Mosaic Covenant was conditional, temporary, and revocable; all of the others are unconditional, irrevocable, permanent, and offered by grace.

Old (Mosaic) Covenant

The Mosaic Covenant, given at Mt. Sinai, is also referred to as the "Old Covenant," a *conditional* agreement between God and the Israelites. The Jews had been living according to the Old Covenant for centuries. The "condition" required them to obey God and keep the law. God, in return, promised to protect and bless them. It was marked by observance of the Sabbath. The outward sign of the covenant was circumcision, applicable only to males.

Due to Israel's repeated violations of the conditions of the Old Covenant, God eventually replaced it with the New Covenant. Our focus will be on the New Covenant, which is closely aligned with the kingdom of God and with the concept of adoption.

The Law and the Hebrew Scriptures

The Hebrew Scriptures were central to the lives of the Jews, from ancient times until present day. They included the Torah and the Oral Torah, the Mishnah, and the Talmud. The Law and the Hebrew Scriptures governed the legal and ethical behaviors of the Jewish people.

Torah refers to the first five books of the Bible, also called the Pentateuch. The Torah is sometimes treated as equivalent to the Scriptures, as a whole. The Oral Torah included the explanations and interpretations of the Pentateuch, as passed down in oral form by rabbis. Many Jews considered the Oral Torah to be as authoritative as the Written Torah.

The Mishnah, created in 200 A.D. captured these oral discussions of Jewish rabbis and scholars (from 200 B.C. through 200 A.D.) in written form.

The Talmud combined the Mishnah with an expansive commentary. The Talmud taught that it was possible for a person to live a sinless life. It also taught that the prophets prophesied only to repentant sinners.

When the rabbis wanted to communicate Scripture, they often used parables. The Greek word *"parabole"* literally meant, "to set beside." The parable invited the listener to compare the presented standard against his own life. (In a way, it was a bit like a very early version of your modern virtual reality game – it invited the reader to place himself inside the story and accept the story as his own.)

Jesus' Parables

There are several features of a parable that are important to understand, in order to grasp the full meaning of the parable.

First of all, a parable is a story -- but a parable is not *just* a story; it is much more! It is a story with a plot built upon everyday objects, used to tell a larger truth. A parable is, at its heart, an extended metaphor. While the story is self-contained within the parable, the parable points to a larger reality (the referent) that lies outside the parable. Typically, for Jesus' parables, that larger reality represented some aspect of the kingdom of God, or his own life and ministry as the Messiah.

Baker's Evangelical Dictionary of Biblical Theology identifies the following important considerations regarding parables:

- *Understand that the parable is an extended metaphor.* Due to its intentionally ambiguous nature, a metaphor (and parable) requires the hearer to "complete" the story by accessing personal details from his own life and experience. Consequently, two people hearing the exact same parable would have different "takeaways" because they brought different backgrounds, beliefs and pre-suppositions to the experience, and those experiences affected how they interpreted the story.

- *Look for the "referent" (i.e., the larger reality)* that supersedes the surface story. In Jesus' parables, the referent was usually the kingdom of God – a novel and unsettling truth, especially for the Pharisees and the teachers of the law!

- *Understand the parable on multiple levels* – first, as Jesus' original hearers' would have understood it, but then move beyond the immediate cultural setting and look for the bigger spiritual reality. This means that you will need to grasp the radical cultural transformation that Jesus brought and look for the kingdom of God message as well as the immediate message.

One of the beauties of parables is their ambiguous nature, which allows them to be tailored to suit a variety of needs, and it requires the hearer to "fill in the blanks" from his own life experience. Thus, different hearers would take away different applications from the same parable.

A parable is both a story and an extended metaphor, but it is also similar to a joke. Just like a joke, a parable was intended to have surprise twists or turns that "catch" the audience. It was that process of being "caught" that made the parable work. The audience was expected to "get" the surprise twists.

One of the biggest problems for modern readers trying to interpret a parable is that we don't have the same background and frame of reference as the original audience; we don't know the "inside jokes". Because modern readers lack much of the cultural background of the parable, we tend to miss a lot of the surprise twists and turns contained within.

If you don't get the punch line to a joke, you really haven't understood the joke. Likewise someone hearing the parable who didn't get the surprise twists or turns in his parable, hadn't "heard" the parable. Much like our modern-day joke, one must have sufficient knowledge of the culture, the idioms, and the times, to get the joke, or to understand the parable. A joke, or a parable, is very culture-dependent.

I'm reminded of a time when I, an American, was working in England for about six months. One Saturday afternoon I had nothing planned, so I decided to go to the local movie theater. The movie playing at the time was *Good Morning, Vietnam!*

I was thoroughly enjoying the movie and laughing out loud when suddenly I realized that I was the only one in the entire theater laughing! Then, when I thought there were a series of "straight lines" ... suddenly, the rest of the people in the theater broke out in laughter. (I saw nothing at all "funny" about those particular lines!)

That movie is a great example of humor that was very culture-specific and time-dependent. If you weren't an American living during the Vietnam era, much of the language and humor would have been lost on you. It really was a case of "you just had to be there" to appreciate the humor ... to get the jokes.

Parables were familiar forms of communication to Jewish audiences because their rabbis had been using them for centuries. They understood how the rabbis included (often implied) references to the Old Testament.

Foreign Domination

Over the centuries, Israel had been controlled by many foreign powers: the Assyrians, the Babylonians, the Persians, the Greeks, and the Romans. The ancient history of Israel can be summarized by five key periods:

1) The Babylonian Exile (or Babylonian Captivity),
2) Resettlement under Persia,
3) Greco-Syrian Oppression,
4) An Eighty Year Period of Independence, and
5) Conflict with Rome.

Throughout these periods of foreign domination, the Jews maintained their separation from those foreign powers through their written and oral laws as well as their observance of the feasts, circumcision, and the Sabbath. It was only when these foreigners tried to suppress their religious practices that the Jews got angry enough to rebel.

Babylonian Captivity (597 B.C. - 581 B.C.)

The Babylonian Exile (or Babylonian Captivity) refers to Nebuchadnezzar II's capture of the Jews and sending them to Babylon. It occurred in three waves from 597 B.C. to 581 B.C. and affected mostly those of the upper class of society (remember Shadrach, Meshach and Abednego?).

Resettlement Under Persia (537 B.C.)

After Cyrus conquered Babylon, he reversed previous religious policy and allowed exiled priests to return to their homelands. In 537 B.C., Cyrus gave the Jews permission to return to Jerusalem.

Greco-Syrian Oppression

Hellenism (332 B.C. – 30 B.C.)

Hellenism became a major influence in the first century. It is generally considered to cover the period from the death of Alexander the Great in 323 B.C. to the incorporation of Egypt into the Roman Empire in 30 B.C.

The Mediterranean culture became Hellenized and remained so throughout the Roman period. Alexander the Great established *koine* Greek as the international language of government, commerce and culture, and he encouraged assimilation of conquered peoples. The Jews, however, believed in maintaining their separate and unique identity; they didn't want to be assimilated into the Greek culture.

One of the primary characteristics of the Greek culture was the existence of an elite, upper class – a stratified social hierarchy. Each level had its well-defined roles, responsibilities and benefits. (Such a stratified society ran counter to Jesus' all-inclusive approach to the kingdom of God, and his encouraging his disciples to be humble slaves and servants.)

Alexander died young, and unfortunately, he left no designated successor, so upon his death, his empire broke into three chunks (Greece, Egypt and Syria), ruled by three of his generals. Initially, Israel fell under the relatively benign governance of the Ptolemaic kingdom (323 B.C. – 30 B.C.).

Antiochus IV Epiphanes Persecuted the Jews (169 B.C. – 167 B.C.)

This benign Greek rule began to change in 198 B.C. when Antiochus III of the Seleucid Empire (312 B.C. - 63 B.C.) conquered the area. The situation worsened with the next Seleucid king, Antiochus IV Epiphanes. He considered the Jews to be the weak link in his defense against the Romans, and he worried because they had not adopted Greek culture. Consequently, he set out to destroy the Jews' religious beliefs as a way of controlling the people.

The Romans were afraid the Jews could gather together and create a rebellion, so they were always on the alert for any hint of rebellion. The Romans reacted strongly to any political threats, and treated the people very harshly.

Forced Hellenism (169 B.C. – 167 B.C.)

Antiochus IV Epiphanes tried to destroy Judaism by forcing the Hellenization of Judaism. He took control of the Temple and corrupted the office of the High Priest. He forbade the observance of Jewish holidays, keeping kosher, studying the Torah, and circumcision. He persecuted, tortured, and killed any Jews who didn't comply. As the final insult, he instituted worship of Greek gods – and swine - in the Temple. (*This was anathema to the Jews!*)

Jewish Independence (166 - 129 BCE)

Following this major desecration of the Temple (Antiochus Epiphanes IV has come to be considered a type of the Antichrist), the Jews staged a revolt, the Maccabean Revolt. It was successful and Israel enjoyed eighty years of independence, until the Romans came along.

Roman Rule (63 B.C. – 313 C.E.)

The Romans had replaced the Seleucids, but they were harsh rulers. King Herod used oppressive taxation, public crucifixion, and torture as ways of controlling the people. Sometimes, the Romans even destroyed entire towns and sold the survivors off into slavery! Herod's building campaigns, and the luxuries in Rome, were financed largely through heavy taxes placed upon the conquered people. The Jews were required to pay taxes to Rome and also, to pay tithes and sacrifices required of their synagogues.

Most of the Jewish people at this time were small peasant farmers, and their heavy tax burden took as much as 50% of their meager incomes. Many of them lost their farms and had to relocate to the more urban areas. The only Jews who prospered were the tax collectors and the corrupt priests, who had sold out to the Romans.

Cultural Background

We need to develop a basic understanding of the culture of first century Israel to appreciate just how radical and revolutionary Jesus' message was. He preached the kingdom of God as the New Covenant, which replaced the Old Mosaic Covenant and was open to all by means of adoption. He claimed to be God and the prophesized Messiah. He encouraged humility servanthood and even depicted himself and his followers as "slaves". He challenged patriarchy and the biological family. He flaunted the Pharisee's burdensome purity and Sabbath rules. All of those teachings ran counter to existing cultural values and created opposition among the people, especially the religious leaders.

Greco-Roman Values

The first century social norms were strongly influenced by Greco-Roman values, especially the shame/honor value system and kinship/patronage. The word "Rome" had a dual character; it represented both a city and an empire. The term "Greek" had a broader connotation. Originally it referred to tribes who spoke the "Hellenes" language and occupied the land now known as Greece. However, after Alexander's conquests, Greek came to mean anyone who had embraced Greek culture. The Romans adopted the Greek language and much of their culture. Because of this blending of cultures, separating the impacts of the two groups was difficult and the hybridized culture came to be known as "Greco-Roman".

Shame/Honor

The Greco-Roman shame-honor based value system was pervasive; it governed almost every activity of everyday life. It affected everything from whom you could talk with to where you could sit at a dinner table. The attainment of honor and avoidance of shame were so important that some considered honor more important than life itself. People did everything possible to gain honor and avoid shame. (These values conflict with Jesus' teachings on humility and servanthood.)

Incurring shame could result in such severe consequences that it was considered a social catastrophe: loss of acceptance, work, friendships and other relationships, and even loss of life. Anyone who failed to abide by societal norms or actively opposed them, was rejected and isolated, shamed and kicked out of the community. Sometimes this excommunication was accompanied with a public beating or stoning.

By the time of Jesus, the Stoics had elevated honor to a very high level. Gentile rulers like Caesar and Herod tended to "lord it over" others; the quest for glory became the highest value in public life. The Romans became quite skilled at publishing and reinforcing their social status through clothing, occupations, seating at banquets or events, and through the legal system.

Stratified Society

Hellenistic society was very stratified; each person in each level of society was expected to know his or her role, responsibilities and benefits. Self-magnification was the central feature of Hellenic higher education.

Kinship / Patronage System

The kinship/patronage system fell under the shame/honor system. It provided a means for an individual to establish self-respect and at the same time be recognized by the group as being a valuable member of the group. Kinship was based on bloodlines and/or arranged relationships. It provided safety, security, as well as opportunity to find a benefactor (patron). Loyalty to family and/or the benefactor were the most important values. (The issues of self-respect and being recognized as a valuable person come into play in the development of the characters in the parable.)

Patronage was a system of public and private favors between patrons (benefactors) and their client (recipient). Under patronage, a wealthy, important, connected individual could become a patron to someone of lesser status. The client was obligated to act in a way that increased the patron's honor (or at a minimum, didn't bring dishonor). At the same time, it raised the client's status and thus, increased his honor.

Grace

Grace did exist as a concept in Israel; however, it was not a religious term, it belonged to the patronage realm. Under patronage, grace came with a price; there was always an obligation to return the favor. It also required faith that the benefactor's promises would be carried out and the client's gratitude would be appropriately expressed. The greater the gift; the greater was the client's obligation of gratitude. Unlike honor, grace could not be earned – it could only be granted.

The Septuagint (300 B.C. – 200 B.C.)

One of the major Grecian influences on the Jews was the development of the Septuagint, the first Greek translation of Hebrew Scriptures, in 300-200 B.C. It contained the 39 books of the Old Testament (as we know them today) plus some apocryphal books, although these were never quoted by any of the New Testament authors. The Septuagint became a popular translation of the Hebrew Scriptures, especially for Hellenized Jews, Greeks, and other Gentiles.

Patriarchy

Family-Centric

Unlike western societies where the individual is the focus, family was the center in the Middle Eastern society. The typical patriarchal family was an extended, multi-generational one, consisting of a male head, one or more wives and concubines (polygamy was an accepted practice in ancient times), children, grandparents and grandchildren, slaves and servants, other relatives and sometimes, even non-related parties.

Such a household could easily include fifty or sixty members. Given the size of these families, roles were clearly defined within a strict hierarchical structure, based upon shame and honor values. Loyalty to family was paramount. (Jesus taught that loyalty to the kingdom of God had to be the number one priority, and it superseded loyalty to one's natural family.)

Male Headship

The Israelite society was patriarchal, but not strictly so. In the strictest sense of patriarchy, men controlled the entire society, and women were excluded from any role in the community; however, Jewish women had some freedom and responsibility, especially within the home.

A male adult ruled the family or clan and represented the family to the community. Generally, a man's honor derived from his land, his possessions and his family. The identity of the family was closely tied to its ownership of real estate. The patriarch's honor extended to all those who were under his protection: women, children, and other dependents. In some circles, the Jewish patriarch was considered a symbol for God.

Only men could win and defend the honor of their family; women and children had no honor of their own. (Women did have honor regarding their sexual purity; however, that was replaced by shame in the event of rape or even consensual relations. Only the patriarch could avenge such shame.)

The Patriarch

The patriarch was like the hub of a wheel; roles, relationships and responsibilities were all defined relative to him. The patriarch had absolute control over the family. He was the highest rank, and was therefore, the most honored member of the family. One of his primary responsibilities was to maintain the family's standard of living and social standing – or increase it, if possible. (A patriarchal father's financial responsibilities are an issue in the story of the man with two sons.)

Eldest Son

The eldest son also had responsibilities to assist his father in hospitality and hosting duties and to be a mediator in times of family conflict. In the event of his father's death, he would become head of the household and become responsible for the wellbeing of his mother, any unmarried sisters and any other children in the home. (The elder son's responsibilities are relevant to the third story of our parable.)

Jewish inheritance rights were governed by the rules of patriarchy, and specifically, by the rules of primogeniture. Those laws were intended to keep control of all lands and property in the hands of the Jews (and the specific tribe). Normally, the firstborn son would be entitled to a double share – but none of this inheritance would be distributed until the death of the patriarch. (The question of inheritance rights and procedures are an important background consideration in this parable.)

Low Status of Women

A Jewish woman had little authority of her own unless she was an heiress in a family with no sons. Regardless of her age, she would have been treated much like a minor child and considered "property". Before marriage, she was considered to be the property of her father's household. Once betrothed, she became the property of her fiancé (even before she physically joined his household).

After marriage, the wife never became a full-fledged member of her husband's family because she could be divorced at any time (and wives frequently were). Laws regarding divorce and adultery favored the man; the woman was at a serious disadvantage. The Torah gave the right of divorce only to the husband, thus giving him tremendous power in the marriage. It also gave the father, or the husband, the right to annul even vows a woman made to God (Num. 30:31).

At best, a woman was always under the control of either her father or husband, but if neither were present, she was extremely vulnerable as an unattached female. (Both Jesus and Luke challenged the low status of women, with Jesus welcoming them into the kingdom as full-fledged members and using a woman as a God-symbol in the second story of this parable.)

Low Status of Children

Children existed for the sake of the family – effectively, for the sake of the parents (Ex. 20:12). The striking of a parent (Ex. 21:15) or even habitual rebelliousness (Deut. 21:18–21) was grounds for the death sentence. Sons frequently followed their father's trade or occupation. Jesus also raised the status of children by using them as examples of the attitude needed to enter the kingdom of God.

Chapter 2

JESUS' WORLD – FIRST CENTURY ISRAEL

When Jesus began his public ministry, there were numerous social, political and religious factions vying for power and influence. It was a time of great change – and great pressure.

Jewish – Roman Conflict

The Jews lived in a Hellenistic culture, which offered prestige and influence to those who adapted. A wide gap developed between the ruling elite (and those who cooperated with them) and the rest of the populace. Political and spiritual passions ran high; the tensions between the Hellenistic culture and Jewish beliefs were pervasive and even dangerous.

Jewish - Roman Cultural Differences

The Jews and the Romans had major cultural differences, which exacerbated the already tense situation between the two groups. The Roman religion was pluralistic, with many gods (renamed Greek gods), emperor worship, and various mystery religions; whereas the Jews' religion was monotheistic.

In addition, there were a number of Greco-Roman philosophies prevalent in first century Israel. Among the more common ones were:

Stoicism, the study of astrology, Gnosticism and the mystery religions. Astrology was widespread and impacted nearly every religion or religious philosophy. Gnosticism was a diversified and complex belief that interacted with both Judaism and early Christianity.

The Romans had a different sense of time, history and even what it meant to be a human person. For the Jews, the Law and the Sabbath were sacred and governed their day-to-day lives; for the Romans, religion played only a minor role in their everyday lives, and they considered the Sabbath merely reflected laziness.

Hellenistic Jews

The Greco-Roman shame/honor system exerted great pressure on many Jews to abandon their religious heritage in favor of the benefits of assimilating Greco-Roman culture and values. The Greek culture had become so pervasive that a number of Jews had become "Hellenized" and were referred to as "Hellenistic Jews."

Hellenistic Judaism was a form of Judaism that combined Jewish tradition with Greek culture. Hellenization of the Jews would have included the use of the Greek language instead of Hebrew and Aramaic, the adoption of Greek names, deviation from traditional Jewish teachings, and syncretism, as well as involvement in many Greek literary and cultural pursuits. This meant, however, that those "Hellenized" Jews had to give up some of their central teachings and religious practices. The Sadducees were quite willing to incorporate Greek culture; whereas the Pharisees were not.

Caesar Augustus (Octavian), Emperor

Caesar Augustus (aka Octavian) was the emperor at the time of Jesus' birth (Luke 2); he controlled the area from 27 B.C. until his death in 14 A.D. He was the one who called for the census that required Joseph and Mary to travel to Bethlehem.

Octavian was considered to be a wise ruler, but his successors were not. Even though Octavian was hailed as a peacemaker, he governed through fear. He worked with powerful local leaders to influence the Jews. He appointed client rulers who administered the conquered territories on his behalf. In 40 B.C., the land became a Roman province.

King Herod

During the civil war in the Roman Empire, Herod had found favor with Octavian. As a result of his political connections, Herod became King of Judea in 37 B.C., and he was given great autonomy. Although Herod tried to win the Jews over through massive building campaigns (including restoration of the Jewish Temple), he never succeeded.

He ruled from 37 B.C. through the time of Jesus, one of the most powerful rulers in the entire Roman Empire, but he was an evil man.

The Jews Hated the Romans

The Jews hated the Romans because of their onerous taxes and their frequent use of torture. The memory of their previous foreign occupations was burned deep into their collective psyches, and those memories dictated much of their response to their current situation in Jesus' day.

Rome was an urban center with Greek culture. The Roman lifestyle was luxurious by most standards – but it was funded on the backs of the conquered peoples through heavy taxation. Most of the Jews were peasant farmers, eking out a living growing olives, figs, grains, dates, and vineyards. There was a wide gap between the upper crust and the typical Jewish family.

After Octavian defeated Rome's enemies, he was celebrated as a great peacemaker and even, "savior". When his deeds were proclaimed throughout the land, people used the Greek term *"euangelion"* meaning "good news" or gospel. This became known as "imperial theology;" the worship of the emperor as divine. Emperor worship became common throughout the land. People praised him for freedom, justice, peace and salvation.

Romans Feared Jewish Rebellion

The Romans were afraid the Jews could gather together and create a rebellion, so they were always on the alert for any hint of rebellion. (The Jews did resist through frequent insurrections.) They reacted strongly to any political threat against their government, and treated the people very harshly. For example, in 4 B.C., the Romans squashed a rebellion in Sepphoris, the provincial capital near Nazareth, by burning it to the ground and selling the survivors into slavery.

Jewish – Gentile Conflict

Jews Hated the Gentiles

The Jews hated the Gentiles because of their pagan religions, involving illicit sex and idolatry. The Jews feared they would be contaminated by those practices. Jews considered the Gentiles to be "unclean," and called them "dogs." Gentiles, and the Samaritans especially, were considered enemies to be shunned, and they were denied knowledge of God unless they became proselytes. Further, the Jews remembered the forced Hellenization of Antiochus IV Epiphanes in 169 B.C.

The Jews were so afraid of Gentile pagan religions that they prohibited all interaction with the Gentiles. The fanatics believed that heretics, traitors, and Jewish "defectors" should be punished. In addition, they believed that a returning heretic should be put to death immediately – partly to atone for his guilt and partly to prevent future betrayals.

Kezazah Shame Ceremony

The Jewish community developed a special "Kezazah" (or cutting-off ceremony) for any Jewish man, who lived with Gentiles and then lost his money to Gentiles (exactly what the younger son did in the third story of our parable). Any young man who lost his fortune this way and then dared to return to his community faced this "shame ceremony".

Because of the hatred of the Jews for the Gentiles, this was considered a particularly shameful act. The village elders would greet the returnee at the edge of the village and break a pot filled with burned corn in front of him, while shouting "{Name} is cut off from his people." Everyone in the community would shun him after that ceremony; no one would have anything to do with him.

Conflict Within Judaism

Not only did the Jews hate the Romans and the Gentiles, there was significant conflict within Judaism itself. During the first century, there were many competing sects and schools. The most prominent were the Pharisees, the Sadducees, the Essenes and the Zealots. In addition, there were the ordinary Jewish people who lived simple lives, following the traditions of their ancestors.

The beliefs and practices of the four major groups differed significantly on keys issues, resulting in infighting and conflict among them.

The Pharisees Separated from Other Jews

The Pharisees, who were known as "Separatists," were the largest and most powerful religious group. (Their importance is clear since they are mentioned 98 times in the New Testament.)

The scholarly Pharisees were experts regarding the law. They believed that the Exile had been caused by their ancestor's failure to keep the law. They added many trivial rules to the law, which became very burdensome to the Jews. The Pharisees were very legalistic and very judgmental of those they considered beneath them (everyone). They were especially dogmatic concerning observance of the Sabbath, food purity rules, and the festivals. They opposed Roman authority when it conflicted with the Law. They accepted the Law, the Prophets and the Writings; they believed in angels, demons, and in the resurrection of the dead.

They were very pious and self-righteous, and they even considered themselves above God (Matt. 23:18-19). They were very concerned with receiving praise and honor. As keepers of the oral law, they became Jesus' chief opponents. (The Apostle Paul was a Pharisee and one of the most aggressive persecutors of early Christians.)

The Sadducees Opposed the Pharisees

The Sadducees, aristocratic priests, were the next most important religious group, but they were despised as collaborators with Rome because they controlled the Temple worship and adopted Hellenism. They were priests, born into the priesthood family, but unlike the Pharisees, they accepted only the written law. They consistently opposed the Pharisees, both religiously and politically. They denied the existence of spirits, angels, the soul, the afterlife, and the resurrection.

The Essenes Thought the Sadducees Had Defiled the Temple

Doctrinally, the Essenes fell between the Pharisees and the Sadducees. They believed the rest of the Jews had abandoned God's path and that the Sadducees had defiled the temple. Like the Pharisees, the Essenes were very concerned with purity, especially the holiness of the Temple. Like the Sadducees, they claimed to be true priests of God, but they took an even stricter view of the purity rules than the Pharisees.

Many of their members lived relatively normal lives within the towns and villages, but kept to themselves. Some of their leaders, however, left the villages and isolated themselves in the Qumran area. They were also very apocalyptic, looking forward to the return of the Messiah.

The Zealots Believed the Priests Should Rule

The Zealots were the most militant of all four groups and overtly resisted Roman rule. They believed that the priests should rule in the name of God, and that Jews should neither acknowledge the emperor as their ruler nor pay taxes to Rome.

The Zealots, the so-called "Fourth Sect," were off in their own little world. Whereas the Sadducees tried to live a good life while seeking powerful positions, the Pharisees sought to live where God had put them but remain pure, and the Essenes simply left the field, the Zealots wanted to change the world. They were willing to confront any opposition directly and violently, if necessary. They were very passionate about their beliefs (hence the name, Zealots).

The Zealots didn't interpret the law; they just defended it. They had three core beliefs: 1) Yahweh was the only king the Jews should acknowledge, 2) They would establish his reign by rooting out paganism and by breaking the yoke of tyranny, and 3) The Torah made separation from the Gentiles necessary, exalted Israel as the chosen of God, and promised triumph.

The Four Jewish Groups Had Major Differences

There were significant differences among these four Jewish sects. The Sadducees were priests and aristocrats, whereas the Pharisees were commoners. The Sadducees were pro-Hellenism, the Pharisees were selective about it, and the Essenes were opposed. The Sadducees believed in free will, the Pharisees were lukewarm about free will, and the Essenes did not believe in it. The Pharisees believed that the Oral Torah was as important as the written Torah, but the Sadducees believed only in the written Torah, and the Essenes believed in "inspired exegesis". The Sadducees did not believe in any kind of an afterlife, the Pharisees believed in the resurrection, while the Essenes believed only in a spiritual survival.

The Zealots and the Essenes were looking for a Messiah who would be a military conqueror and establish God's kingdom on earth right away. They wanted war, vengeance, and a king who would destroy their enemies. The Pharisees and later rabbis believed the Messiah couldn't arrive until the entire nation of Israel was living according to God's law.

Because of these major points of disagreement among the four Jewish sects, it's no wonder they had difficulties getting along with one another.

CHAPTER 3

WHO IS THIS JESUS?

The Jews had longed for a Messiah for centuries, and suddenly Jesus appeared among them, claiming to be that Messiah. They were looking for a military leader and a king who would overthrow their oppressive Roman rulers. The Jews didn't accept Jesus as the Messiah because he did not fit their expectations.

Many of them were confused or even angry. Just who was this guy? Should they listen to him – or stone him?

Jesus' Birth

Jesus was born of humble parents, in a manger in Bethlehem because the Roman ruler had mandated a census, which required Joseph and Mary to travel to Bethlehem. The wise men following Jesus' birth star unwittingly set off a chain of events alerting King Herod to the birth of "the king of the Jews."

Jesus at the Temple

The next time we heard of Jesus, he was at the Temple. His parents had already left Jerusalem before they realized he was not with them. They returned to Jerusalem and found twelve year-old Jesus at the Temple, amazing the priests with his knowledge (Luke 2:41-52).

Jesus' Baptism

Jesus' baptism, by John the Baptist, marked the beginning of his public ministry. John's baptism was for repentance, and even though Jesus had never sinned, he underwent this baptism to identify with the sinners he came to save. Jesus' baptism was the first occurrence of the Trinity appearing to men: Jesus was baptized and his Father spoke aloud. Others (including John) heard his words and saw the Holy Spirit descend like a dove:

> When all the people were being baptized, Jesus was baptized too. And as he was praying, heaven was opened [22] and the Holy Spirit descended on him in bodily form like a dove. And a voice came from heaven: "You are my Son, whom I love; with you I am well pleased." (Luke 3:21-23)

Jesus Tempted in the Wilderness

Immediately after his baptism, the Holy Spirit led Jesus into the wilderness to be tempted by Satan (Luke 4:1-13). Jesus defeated Satan on all points, and did not succumb to sin. During the time in the wilderness, Jesus came face-to-face with his enemy and learned exactly what he was going to be pitted against. It also solidified his identity as the Messiah.

From that point forward, he moved with greater confidence and awareness of his mission and his identity as the Messiah, empowered by the Holy Spirit.

Jesus Was a Learned Rabbi

We tend to think of Jesus as a carpenter – and he was; he was a skilled craftsman. But, he was also a learned scholar who amazed people with his knowledge and understanding, from a very young age. Throughout his public ministry Jesus demonstrated knowledge and wisdom comparable to the rabbis.

Even the Pharisees (who hated Jesus) acknowledged him as "rabbi," which was a term of respect.

Jesus Used Parables

Like many rabbis before him, Jesus used parables. Parables were central to his ministry; approximately one-third of his teachings utilized parables. Jesus used parables to accomplish many objectives, but chief among them were to: reveal (and conceal) his identity and the kingdom of God, to demonstrate God's sovereignty, to force a decision about his message, and to separate believers from unbelievers.

CHAPTER 4

JESUS' REVOLUTIONARY MISSION AND MINISTRY

After having experienced so many years of oppression and injustice, the Jews longed for the promised Messiah; they looked forward to a king who would free from their oppressors and establish his kingdom on earth. They were tired, frustrated, and they hated the Roman oppression. Each day that went by increased their longing for the Messiah to appear, but many were going to be disappointed by this Jesus. Jesus' ministry was quite a shock to the Jews. They were expecting him to overthrow the Romans, **not to confront them** about their own sins.

Jesus' Mission

Jesus claimed to be the Messiah and God; however, "Messiah Jesus" differed significantly from Jewish expectations of the promised Messiah. Jesus was a radical revolutionary who didn't fit Jewish expectations, and he didn't support the status quo. His ministry produced quite an upheaval in first century Israel.

In its simplest form, Jesus' mission consisted of two things:

1) Preach the kingdom of God, and
2) Seek and save the lost.

Preach the Kingdom of God

Jesus described his mission saying that he *"must preach the good news of the kingdom of God"* (Luke 4:43). Because of the seriousness of his mission, Jesus didn't mince words and he didn't waste time. Jesus knew exactly who he was, what he came to do, and what it would cost him (his life) to be successful in his mission.

Seek and Save the Lost

In Luke 15, Jesus had just been criticized for eating with "sinners." He responded by affirming his mission was to save the people who needed saving; their sinfulness was the very reason to seek them out, not shun them as the Pharisees and other religious leaders, did. He told them, *"For the Son of Man came to seek and to save the lost."* (Luke 19:10)

Jesus Was Controversial

You may not have realized it before, but Jesus was very controversial and politics were central to his ministry. From the very beginning, Jesus' life was entangled with politics. Starting with his birth announcement all the way through his norm-shattering ministry, Jesus rocked the political boat. He was political and confrontational when he talked about the kingdom of God; he could have used much less confrontational language, but he chose not to do so.

Jesus' Birth Challenged Imperial Theology

Jesus' ministry was quite controversial, but amazingly, even his birth created quite a stir in the Roman world – and it would have created an even bigger one had the emperor heard the angels' announcement to the shepherds! Jesus' birth announcement to the shepherds was a direct challenge to imperial theology (Luke 2:10-11). The angels' language claimed that Jesus - not the emperor - was the true king who would bring peace on earth.

Herod became convinced that Jesus was a threat to his throne, so he decided to kill Jesus while he was still an infant. When Herod couldn't accomplish the assassination of one small baby, he ordered the slaughter of all Jewish boys under the age of two, in the entire Bethlehem area – all because he felt threatened – by a baby! Herod, unknowingly, fulfilled two Old Testament prophecies with his horrendous actions (Jer. 31:15, Hos. 11:1). Some accounts say 14,000 babies were killed!

As this was happening, an angel warned Joseph of Herod's evil plan, so Mary and Joseph fled Egypt and did not return until after Herod had died:

> When they had gone, an angel of the Lord appeared to Joseph in a dream. "Get up," he said, "take the child and his mother and escape to Egypt. Stay there until I tell you, for Herod is going to search for the child to kill him." (Matt. 2:13)

Jesus Antagonized the Pharisees

Jesus criticized the Pharisees for their pride and hypocrisy, and he trivialized their purity and Sabbath rules which placed excessive burdens on the people. In Matthew 23, alone, he called them "hypocrites" seven times, "blind guides" twice, "fools and blind" twice, "blind" once, "whitewashed tombs" once and "finally, "brood of vipers." And, finally, he pronounced seven woes upon them.

Although the scribes and the Pharisees were technically two separate groups, they were both legal experts, and consequently, they tended to get lumped together. For example, when Jesus issued his "Seven Woes" statement, he addressed it to both the scribes and the Pharisees.

The Pharisees and Religious Leaders Hated Jesus

The Pharisees hated Jesus because they saw him as a threat to their power base, and they considered his claim to be God blasphemy. Jesus claimed to be a king, a prophet, the Messiah, and God. Many times during his ministry, he forgave sinners and unclean people that the self-righteous leaders of the day shunned.

His message was very disruptive to the status quo. By the time he died, the scribes (Mk. 2:6-7), the teachers of the law (Mk. 12:38), the Priests (Mk. 14:55), and the Pharisees (Mk. 2:16) all hated him.

Jesus' Message Was Revolutionary

Jesus' Message Was Divisive

Jesus was a very divisive force in first century Israel. His message riled both the political and religious leaders, especially the Pharisees. It divided families, clans and kinship networks. His message forced people to make a decision and choose sides; there was no "sitting on the fence". Jesus challenged many of the underpinnings of traditional Jewish life and brought massive disruptive changes to their world. He simply didn't fit their expectations. Jesus:

- Brought division, not peace.
- Confronted the Pharisees regarding their leadership failure.
- Replaced the Old Covenant with the New Covenant and the kingdom of God.
- Confronted legalism and hypocrisy.
- Challenged the Jewish view of God.
- Claimed to be God.
- Confronted Messianic Expectations.
- Introduced the kingdom family.
- Challenged the shame/honor value system.
- Challenged kinship/patronage.
- Challenged patriarchy.
- Elevated the low status of women.
- Challenged adultery laws.

- Challenged divorce laws.
- Replaced inheritance with adoption.
- Offered people a new identity.

Jesus, like John the Baptist before him, called people away from legalistic and pharisaical Judaism to a New Covenant and the kingdom of God. He offered them a new life and adoption into the kingdom family.

Jesus Challenged Jewish View of God

Jesus Claimed to Be God

In our parable Jesus portrayed himself as God using the following images: a shepherd, a woman, a father and a younger son. In doing so, he communicated that the patriarchal view of God was inadequate; he broadened their view of God by including feminine and caring attributes as part of God's essential nature and by incorporating an active seeking and saving component to his character as well. According to Baker's Evangelical Dictionary of the Bible, *"Of Jesus' fifty-two recorded narrative parables, twenty seem to depict him in imagery that in the Old Testament metaphorical use typically referred to God."* For example,

- Jesus said that he and the Father were one (John 10:30).
- He said he existed before Abraham, using the same words God used with Moses from the burning bush (John 8:58, Ex. 3:14).
- He claimed that anyone who had seen him had seen the Father. (John 14:9)

Adoption, Not Legalism

Not only did Jesus refer to God as Father, but he also used the intimate, relational word, *"abba"* to do so (which the Jews never did). Jesus invited his followers to move from a master-slave paradigm to a much more intimate father-son (or father-daughter) relationship with God. He authorized them to use the same intimate address for God that he used thus solidifying their familial relationship (Rom. 8:14ff; Gal. 4:4–7). That was a radical change to the Jewish view of God. The added dimension of adoption further alienated the Pharisees because it allowed people considered unclean or unworthy to become members of God's family.

Kingdom of God Parables

Jesus' parables spoke to the kingdom of God and the New Covenant as replacing the Old Mosaic Covenant. His parables reflected his person and mission. Tenney pointed out that a person's response to Jesus' parables reflected that person's response to Jesus and to the kingdom of God.

Many authors suggest that *some* of Jesus' parables are kingdom parables and other parables are not; however, following Edersheim, I suggest that they are *all* kingdom parables. Edersheim breaks Jesus' parables into three groups, spoken at three different periods in the history of Christ, and marking three different stages in the opposition of the Pharisees.

The first set (Matthew 13) addresses the Pharisees' contention that Jesus' ministry was demonic. Jesus responded by explaining basic truths about the kingdom of God, its development and reality.

The second series (Luke 10–16, 18) occurred after the Transfiguration. These parables also address the kingdom of God, but their tone is more controversial and they react to direct opposition of the kingdom, especially from the Pharisees. *The Luke 15 parable falls in this group.*

The third series (Matthew 18, 20–22, 24, 25, Luke 19), which occurred shortly before Jesus' rejection and betrayal, is the most controversial, even judgmental. The kingdom of God is the harvest stage.

Parables Helped Him Control Timing

Jesus used figurative and ambiguous language in his parables. He did that so that his followers could understand his message, but his enemies would not.

What was so special about his mission and ministry that he had to disguise it in parables? Jesus' message, and his overall ministry, were political, controversial, and created opposition among the religious leaders. He was a revolutionary who turned the world upside-down. If he hadn't disguised his message in parables, his enemies might have turned him over to the Roman authorities and crucified him "before it was time."

None of the rulers of this age understood it, for if they had, they would not have crucified the Lord of glory. (I Cor. 2:8)

Jesus had a superb sense of timing and maintained firm control over his schedule. He knew it was too early to be taken into custody, since not all the required prophecies had been fulfilled. Using parables was just one more way that Jesus maintained control over his public ministry.

Not only was Jesus' ministry radical and transformative, it was divisive as well. This divisiveness was a central feature of his parables – and an intentional one. He used parables consistently to divide people into two groups or two paths: believers vs. unbelievers, sinners vs. the self-righteous, those who wanted to entrap him vs. those who wanted to hear his message. He forced his audience to choose – one path or the other.

Many people think of Jesus as a very forgiving and compassionate person (which he was) but they overlook his divisive message. Jesus said,

I have come to bring fire on the earth … Do you think I came to bring peace on earth? No, I tell you, but division … (Luke 12:49)

People Responded to Jesus' Parables Like They Responded to Him

Jesus' parables called people to a new life in the kingdom of God, but it was an "either-or" choice. They couldn't be both Jewish (by religion) and a follower of Jesus; the two were mutually exclusive. Tenney pointed out that an individual's response to Jesus' parables reflected his response to Jesus and to the kingdom of God:

Jesus bears testimony to his own person and mission, albeit in veiled form, so that the hearer's response to the parable is their response to the kingdom of God and to Jesus himself.

The key question became *"Who do you say that I am?"* And, there was only one right answer to that question — Jesus was the Messiah, not just a prophet, or a great teacher or rabbi; he was God; he was the promised Messiah. They had to choose.

Suffering Servant

Jesus willingly — and repeatedly — positioned himself as a servant or slave. Jesus taught his followers that they needed to shift from looking for the Messiah who would be a conquering hero and overthrow the Roman government to a Messiah who was a suffering servant. (All of this teaching was so contrary to the shame/honor paradigm and the self-magnification mindset of the day.) Even Jesus, the "Son of Man," a powerful messianic ruler (Dan 7:14) applied the terms servant and slave to himself. He came to serve, and that's what he did; he healed the sick, the blind, and the leper.

Jesus compounded the problem by claiming that he would offer his life as a ransom - the price paid to release a slave or captive from bondage. He associated with tax collectors and sinners. He welcomed Gentiles. He treated women with respect.

It was inevitable that his servanthood would involve suffering. Suffering and death were necessary for Jesus to provide salvation for sinners. Adopting the position of slave or servant and being the ransom for others was perhaps Jesus' most counter-cultural move of all, and his humble attitude led right into Jesus' death on the cross. In promoting the concepts of humility and servanthood, Jesus was requiring his followers to shift from pride and self-aggrandizement to love and service.

Unfortunately, many of those who most desperately longed for the coming Messiah failed to recognize him when he arrived because he didn't fit within their expectations. All previous history had been looking forward to this moment in history -- this arrival of Christ the Messiah.

Jesus Challenged Jewish Culture

Jesus Challenged Patriarchy and the Family

Jesus was born under the laws and patriarchal culture of the Old Testament but he challenged them on many points. Jesus insisted that the kingdom of God be his disciples' number one priority; nothing else (including family obligations or loyalty) could interfere with Jesus' call on their life or overturn the priority of the kingdom (Mark 3:20–35). Jesus taught his followers:

> *If anyone comes to me without hating his father and mother, wife and children, brothers and sisters, and even his own life, he cannot be my disciple. (Luke 14:26)*

He made this point even more strikingly when he told a potential disciple to let the dead bury the dead; he was needed to proclaim the kingdom of God (Luke 9:60). A son's responsibility to his family - and to his dead father - would have been significant under patriarchy, yet Jesus told this man that he had a much higher loyalty and a higher calling. His familial responsibilities paled in comparison to the call of the kingdom of God and had to be set aside to follow Jesus. Countryman says:

> *Jesus' teaching in the Gospels, sharply diminishes the role, importance and internal stability of the family. By treating women as equals in sexual ownership and by taking children as symbols of citizenship in the Reign of God, Jesus undercuts the role of the patriarch, which was the organizing principle of household life among both Jews and Gentiles.*

Also, by setting the call of discipleship in opposition to the family and its obligations, he radically subordinates family as such to the Reign of God.

Jesus was not promoting "hate;" rather he was merely establishing priorities. He was teaching his followers about priorities in the kingdom of God. Jesus taught that his disciples had to place the kingdom of God as their number one priority above all else, including their family of origin. He undercut the role of the patriarch by elevating the status of women. This was a radical departure from the cultural norms of the day.

What an upheaval that would have caused in a patriarchal household!

Kingdom Family

Jesus replaced the natural family with those who heard God's word and put it into practice (Luke 8:19-21). Jesus insisted that the kingdom of God take top priority in one's life. Jesus included people in the kingdom of God through adoption, not family, kin or tribal relationships. He even included those whom the religious leaders called "sinners" and "unclean," such as the tax collectors.

When Jesus gave his disciples the Lord's Prayer, he authorized them to use that same intimate address for God. This is considered clear evidence of your adoption through Christ as sons (Rom. 8:14ff; Gal. 4:4-7). Extending this right to the church, as a whole, fulfills God's promise, *"I will be a Father to you, and you will be my sons and daughters, says the Lord Almighty."* (2 Cor. 6:18)

Jesus Replaced Inheritance with Adoption

He completed the affront by creating a new kingdom of God family and calling his followers "brothers and sisters." He would even go so far as to call servants and slaves "brothers and sisters." This was quite shocking to the people. He said, *here are my mother and my brothers. For whoever does the will of God is my brother and sister and mother. (Mark 3:34–35)*

One of the specific changes Jesus implemented was to replace patriarchy with adoption. God adopts someone purely by his sovereign choice, just because of his great love. He does not "need" anyone, but he chooses to share his love and joy. No longer was bloodline or birth order or sex sufficient to guarantee a place in the kingdom of God.

The Westminster Confession defines adoption as follows:

*"… adoption is considered the highest blessing because of the rich relationship with God that it engenders. Adoption is a **family** idea, conceived in terms of **love**, and viewing God as **father**. In adoption, God takes you into His family and fellowship, and establishes s as His children and heirs. Closeness, affection and generosity are at the heart of the relationship. To be right with God the judge is a great thing, but to be loved and cared for by God the father is a greater."*

According to Greek tradition, the adopted child incurred legal obligations and moral/religious duties to the new family as well. Thus, he accepted an entirely new set of values and more as well. According to Leitch, **"In the Greek tradition**, *adoption was conditional upon the son's acceptance of the legal obligations and religious duties of the father."*

Adoption is a promised inheritance, and therefore, it is a guaranteed reality. But adoption is a gift and it must be accepted by the one being adopted – the "adoptee" must accept the rules and values of the new family. Adoption goes beyond the mere facts of a legal transaction, and emphasizes the conscious, experiential nature of the *relationship*.

Security Defined by Relationship, Not Real Estate

Adoption is a family concept: Jesus always thought of himself as the Son of God and he always thought of his followers as children of his heavenly Father, members of the same divine family as himself.

Security is no longer defined by inheriting a piece of real estate, but rather, by entering into a family relationship with God by means of adoption. The believer's inheritance is now a relationship in the family of God; it is no longer a piece of real estate, and it can never be lost or stolen. God's desire to give his people a secure abode now comes through the kingdom of God and eternal life.

With the coming of the kingdom of God, inheritance rights were granted to all. All who believed could claim their position as heirs of God and joint-heirs with Christ.

Jesus Challenged Low Status of Women

Jesus and Luke both elevated the status of women. By elevating everyone's primary allegiance to God, Jesus also broke down cultural barriers. He welcomed women into the kingdom – without needing husbands, fathers or sons to escort them and manage their lives. He constantly treated them with respect and dignity. He had female friends and even female disciples. Most notably, the news of his resurrection was announced first to the women at the tomb. He ate at their homes and he accepted lavish gifts of oil poured onto his feet from some of the women who followed him.

His teaching required people to make a paradigm shift from women as property to women as beloved daughters of the kingdom.

Jesus Challenged Shame/Honor System

Jesus taught humility and servanthood; he didn't venerate the proud Pharisees, or the powerful patriarch, rather, he taught his disciples to be humble, like little children. To be childlike is the opposite of the proud, judgmental, self-righteous and legalistic Pharisees.

Jesus called people to shift from the shame / honor value system to the kingdom values of humility and servanthood. The honor vs. shame paradigm encouraged people to seek power and prestige, often at the expense of others. It promoted competition, pride and selfishness. Its number one goal was self-magnification.

According to the shame/honor system, only the "honorable" would be allowed to enter into the Temple or be acceptable to God. Not only did Jesus refute that idea, he actively sought out the "undesirables" of society and invited them into the kingdom.

The Pharisees, in particular, had difficulty with this concept – but even Jesus' disciples struggled. For example, James and John, the sons of Zebedee, had a lucrative fishing business, they knew the high priest in Jerusalem, and they had high status. For them to adopt the role of a "slave" would have caused them to lose their position of honor and accept dishonor in its place.

Jesus taught his disciples to give away their money, to be humble like slaves, and to adopt an attitude of servanthood. Being considered a "slave" Is the lowest societal class and even hinted at degradation and abuse. It would have been demeaning and offensive to both Jews and Gentiles alike. That teaching hit at the very heart of that honor vs. shame value paradigm. His use of the terms "slave" and "servant" offended many because they would have had to give up their hard-won status and accept obscurity and shame.

It was common in their culture for someone to incur shame as the result of losing a competition or challenge, but to humble oneself and take on a shameful position *voluntarily* like Jesus did was unheard of. This was one of the reasons the Pharisees objected to Jesus' eating with tax collectors and sinners – they thought it brought dishonor on Jesus, a respected rabbi and teacher, and indirectly, they believed it would also tarnish their image in the community.

These values were diametrically opposed to one another. Under the shame/honor paradigm, one could never rest because honor could be lost and shame incurred at any time through various actions and behaviors, or even cruel circumstances of life. Under the kingdom of God, one could rest based on the eternal security of adoption.

Jesus Confronted Legalism and Hypocrisy

Jesus drove the Pharisees crazy by frequently ignoring their purity rules. Jewish law had placed its emphasis on outward acts and behaviors, and the Pharisees had expanded those rules even further. As one of their first public acts, Jesus and his disciples broke Sabbath by picking heads of grain (Mark 2:23). He got angry and threw the moneychangers out of the Temple (Mark 11:15-19).

In contrast to the Pharisees' legalism, Jesus placed his emphasis on thoughts and attitudes of the heart. Jesus taught that love for God was the basic commandment, closely followed by love for one's neighbor. (Mark 12:28-31) The Pharisees had been overly concerned about what food a person ate (or with whom), or what he touched, but Jesus challenged those outward concerns and shifted the conversation to matters of the heart:

> Are you still so dull?" Jesus asked them. "Don't you see that whatever enters the mouth goes into the stomach and then out of the body? But the things that come out of a person's mouth come from the heart, and these defile them. For out of the heart come evil thoughts—murder, adultery, sexual immorality, theft, false testimony, slander. These are what defile a person; but eating with unwashed hands does not defile them. (Matt. 15:16-20)

Jesus poured out upon the Pharisees a series of seven woes, ending with *"You serpents, you brood of vipers, how are you to escape being sentenced to hell?"* (Matt. 23:33) It was clear what Jesus thought about the Pharisees.

Discipleship Has a Cost

Jesus also called people to a radical new identity and a new way of living. He invited them to become part of the kingdom family of God – without regard to status, wealth or family background. He invited the rich and the poor, men and women, Jews and Gentiles. He called them to a path of discipleship, love and service to others.

There was a high cost to following Jesus. Unlike today, a person couldn't simply switch from one "denomination" to another "denomination." If someone decided to follow Jesus, s/he essentially had to abandon his or her former life, including family. S/he would no longer be called a "Jew," but a follower of Jesus (and later, a "Christian").

Their families would have rejected them. Their Jewish brethren would have considered them heretics or blasphemers as the Pharisees did. Converts may have been completely cut off from their former lives, their biological families, their work, as well as their social network.

In that day, family was everything, and to be cut off from family was, at least to some, a fate worse than death. To become a follower of Jesus was not a decision undertaken likely; the ramifications of such a decision were huge.

Jesus called people to a new spiritual reality and because of that, his parables were inherently divisive. He didn't shy away from that fact, nor did he try to sugarcoat or water-down his message. He challenged, criticized and confronted many facets of existing Judaic religion and culture.

CHAPTER 5

THE LUKE 15 PARABLE

This chapter will introduce the parable Jesus gave in response to criticism from the Pharisees and the teachers of the law, but first, a little background.

Luke's Gospel

This parable is recorded in the "Gospel of Luke," which was written by Luke, one of Paul's traveling companions. Luke was an educated man and wrote for a learned Greek audience. He wrote his gospel in the latter part of the first century, somewhere around 60-70 AD.

Luke directed his gospel to Gentiles who needed encouragement in the faith and who were struggling to get incorporated into the Christian community. Specifically, he wrote to a man named Theophilus, possibly his benefactor.

Luke took a relatively political posture; he gave voice to those who were dissatisfied with Roman rule. Although he tried to allay Rome's fears about the Jews and the Christians, he emphasized that followers of Jesus had a higher loyalty than Rome. In addition, Luke was relatively antagonistic to the Jews because they had rejected the Messiah.

Luke Emphasized the Kingdom of God

One of Luke's primary themes in this gospel is the kingdom of God. Luke mentions the kingdom of God 32 times, more than any of the other Gospel writers. Matthew was a close second at 24, if you count "kingdom of God" and "kingdom of heaven" as synonymous, which most theologians would do.

Luke recognized the two-fold nature of the kingdom of God. He recorded Jesus' declaration that he had initiated the kingdom of God on earth and that the kingdom of God would be fully realized when he returns in glory (Luke 17:30). Jesus taught that the kingdom of God had already come with the authority he demonstrated by his miracles and his forgiveness of sin, but the kingdom of God remained to come in full glory.

Luke Emphasized Certainty

Luke's stated purpose (1:1-4) was to set out *"an orderly account … so that you may know the certainty of the things you have been taught."* The word that Luke uses for "certainty" [*asphaleian*] is a strong word, a beautiful word. It lets his audience know that they can rely on these teachings, *with absolute certainty, security, safety and stability.* It's the same word used of a prison that is securely locked, and therefore, impenetrable. It was used 19 times in the Septuagint, to mean safety.

In other words, Luke is strongly emphasizing the absolute certainty his audience can have in this material: *locked-down, secure, unshakeable, solid, stable and immovable reality.* Luke wanted his audience to be confident in their beliefs, knowing that they will stand the test of time. These teachings are safe and secure, they won't be stolen away, nor will they be changed like the wind.

Jesus As Prophet and Suffering Servant

Luke gradually revealed Jesus as not only the Messiah, but also a prophet like Moses and the suffering servant. By relating Jesus to Moses, Luke was identifying Jesus as the appropriate person to interpret the Law.

As Luke reported Jesus' life and ministry during the Galilean and Perean phases, he portrayed Jesus as the "divine man", and emphasized his miracles. The Perean ministry (9:51–19:27) portrayed Jesus on his way to Jerusalem and emphasized discipleship. The Galilean ministry (4:31–9:50) further emphasized his miraculous or healing activities and showed the growth of Jesus' ministry.

The Complete Parable – Luke 15

The complete parable includes all three stories: the shepherd who lost his sheep, the woman who lost her coin, and the man who had two sons. It provides Jesus' response to the Pharisees who were criticizing him for eating with sinners:

15 Now the tax collectors and sinners were all gathering around to hear Jesus. 2 But the Pharisees and the teachers of the law muttered, "This man welcomes sinners and eats with them."

3 Then Jesus told them this parable:

4 "Suppose one of you has a hundred sheep and loses one of them. Doesn't he leave the ninety-nine in the open country and go after the lost sheep until he finds it? 5 And when he finds it, he joyfully puts it on his shoulders 6 and goes home. Then he calls his friends and neighbors together and says, 'Rejoice with me; I have found my lost sheep.' 7 I tell you that in the same way there will be more rejoicing in heaven over one sinner who repents than over ninety-nine righteous persons who do not need to repent.

8 "Or suppose a woman has ten silver coins and loses one. Doesn't she light a lamp, sweep the house and search carefully until she finds it? 9 And when she finds it, she calls her friends and neighbors together and says, 'Rejoice with me; I have found my lost coin.' 10 In the same way, I tell you, there is rejoicing in the presence of the angels of God over one sinner who repents."

11 Jesus continued: "There was a man who had two sons. 12 The younger one said to his father, 'Father, give me my share of the estate.' So he divided his property between them.

13 "Not long after that, the younger son got together all he had, set off for a distant country and there squandered his wealth in wild living. 14 After he had spent everything, there was a severe famine in that whole country, and he began to be in need. 15 So he went and hired himself out to a citizen of that country, who sent him to his fields to feed pigs. 16 he longed to fill his stomach with the pods that the pigs were eating, but no one gave him anything.

17 "When he came to his senses, he said, 'How many of my father's hired servants have food to spare, and here I am starving to death! 18 I will set out and go back to my father and say to him: Father, I have sinned against heaven and against you. 19 I am no longer worthy to be called your son; make me like one of your hired servants.' 20 So he got up and went to his father.

"But while he was still a long way off, his father saw him and was filled with compassion for him; he ran to his son, threw his arms around him and kissed him.

21 "The son said to him, 'Father, I have sinned against heaven and against you. I am no longer worthy to be called your son.'

22 "But the father said to his servants, 'Quick! Bring the best robe and put it on him. Put a ring on his finger and sandals on his feet. 23 Bring the fattened calf and kill it. Let's have a feast and celebrate. 24 For this son of mine was dead and is alive again; he was lost and is found.' So they began to celebrate.

25 "Meanwhile, the older son was in the field. When he came near the house, he heard music and dancing. 26 So he called one of the servants and asked him what was going on. 27 'Your brother has come,' he replied, 'and your father has killed the fattened calf because he has him back safe and sound.'

28 "The older brother became angry and refused to go in. So his father went out and pleaded with him. 29 But he answered his father, 'Look! All these years I've been slaving for you and never disobeyed your orders. Yet you never gave me even a young goat so I could celebrate with my friends. 30 But when this son of yours who has squandered your property with prostitutes comes home, you kill the fattened calf for him!'

31 'My son,' the father said, 'you are always with me, and everything I have is yours. 32 But you had to celebrate and be glad, because this brother of yours was dead and is alive again; he was lost and is found.'

Jesus' parables used common, everyday elements, having deeper spiritual referents. His parables featured farmers, seeds, weeds, women, coins, fathers, children, and many other common elements. But his parables were not really about these simple elements; he had a bigger truth to tell.

We want to look at the entire parable, as it's recorded in Luke 15, but first, a few housekeeping notes:

- I will avoid using the labels, or headers, that many translations include at the beginning of each of the three stories. I do this for two reasons. First of all, those labels are not part of the original text and secondly, they lead you astray in interpreting the parable.

- I will consider the terms kingdom of God and kingdom of heaven to be synonymous, as do most scholars. Because the Jews would not use the name of God, or include it in any writing, they did not use the term kingdom of God. Rather, they opted for the term kingdom of heaven. Matthew's gospel, directed to a Jewish audience, uses kingdom of heaven instead of kingdom of God.

- Finally, I will seldom refer to the younger son as the "prodigal" because I believe it to be an inaccurate depiction of his character, his heart and his motivation and because the word itself is not found in the original text; it is a later "add-on".

This Parable Is Complex

Our parable is definitely one of the more complex parables Jesus told. The complexities arise from the number of characters, symbols, spiritual referents, locations, and timeframes that are involved. The historical-cultural background reflects a very dynamic world with a variety of tense competing social, political and religious factions. Like most of Jesus' parables, this parable has multiple levels, multiple layers, and multiple meanings. We could easily talk about any number of themes such as sin, repentance, compassion, grace, freedom, etc. Having so many variables involved makes this a very complex parable to analyze.

The Audience

There are two groups present in the audience: 1) the Pharisees and the teachers of the law, and 2) the tax collectors and sinners. They were all gathering around to hear Jesus, but the two groups were very different and they had very different objectives.

The Pharisees and Teachers of the Law

They were scholars responsible the development and preservation of the oral law. They believed that keeping the law both the written law and the oral law was paramount.

They weren't very fond of Jesus; he violated many of their oral laws. In their eyes, he was guilty of breaking the law and of blasphemy. They used every opportunity to make him look bad and discredit his message. This day, they were muttering and grumbling. They thought they had him trapped ... he had the audacity to share a meal with these lowly, unclean, tax collectors. ***How dare he?***

The Pharisees and the teachers of the law were constantly looking for ways to trap Jesus then they could hand him over to the Roman authorities. In this chapter, they raised a criticism (or really, an implied question), challenging Jesus why he ate with sinners, which to them implied that he was condoning sin, making himself unclean, and shaming himself in the process.

In essence, they were asking for him to explain his motivation, to defend his "sinful behavior" (for the Pharisees considered it a "sin" to eat with tax collectors). They considered themselves to be very righteous and consequently, better than everyone else. They were only interested in Jesus and his motivation (15:1-2), and ... a way to make him look bad in front of the crowd; they weren't interested in the sinners.

Since they were asking Jesus to explain himself, we'll focus our attention on the characters in the parable that he used to portray himself. They didn't want to have anything at all to do with the other group for fear that they might become unclean themselves simply by association.

The Tax Collectors and Sinners

The tax collectors and the sinners comprised the second group; you have "all" of them, a lot of them; a crowd. Most people wouldn't have anything to do with them, but here was Jesus not only speaking to them, but actively seeking them out, welcoming them, treating them like real people, and he even ate at some of their homes! Jesus did not just receive sinners; he actively sought them out and eagerly awaited their coming (much like the younger son's father eagerly watched for him to return). He had his eye out for them. (Luke 15:2)

This group was genuinely interested in what Jesus had to say. The tax collectors, who were universally hated, were thrilled that a learned rabbi was speaking directly to them and treating them like real human beings rather than the dregs of the earth (Matt. 11:19). Jesus' message was a dramatic change from that of the rabbis who forbade them entrance into the Temple and wouldn't even accept money from them because they considered it tainted. (The Mishnah taught that they were so impure that they could taint whatever they touched.)

Jesus offered them forgiveness of sins and a new life as a member of the kingdom family. Jesus had even called Mathew to be one of his disciples (Matt. 9:9). The reason Jesus had been eating with the tax collectors (Mark 2) was that Matthew wanted to celebrate with his friends and introduce them to Jesus. Not only did Jesus talk to the tax collectors, and eat with them, he sought them out.

When he entered Jericho and encountered Zacchaeus, a wealthy chief tax collector and asked to stay at Zacchaeus' house, he bypassed about 12,000 priests in the city of Jericho to stay with a lowly tax collector! No wonder the "elite" were upset, Jesus had just snubbed them by visiting tax collector's home but not theirs!

Although the interests of the Pharisees and the tax collectors were diametrically opposed, Jesus was able to speak to both groups at the same time through his masterful use of parables. That would be a tremendous challenge for any speaker of any day and age! But Jesus was a masterful communicator, and he rose to the occasion by responding with the following parable.

The Timing of This Parable

Jesus gave this parable about midway into his public ministry. When Jesus began his public ministry, he didn't use many parables; his speech was much more straightforward and clear-cut. As time went on, however, and opposition to his ministry grew, Jesus altered his approach and increasingly used parables as his preferred method of communication.

Three Stories, One Parable

Jesus responded to the Pharisees' criticism with three stories: the story of the shepherd who had one hundred sheep, the story of the woman who had ten coins, and the story of the man who had two sons.

When responding to the Pharisees' criticism, verse three says: "*Then Jesus told them **this** parable*" (singular, not "these three parables"). In order for Jesus to provide an acceptable answer to the Pharisees' concern, his answer had to match the essential part of the question – not some tangential point.

Since he told three stories in order to answer the criticism, we must look for the common themes across all three stories – the ones that would be responsive to the criticism. *We know that Jesus' answer (i.e., the parable) required all three stories because Jesus said so.*

These three pictures reveal a lot about the character of God, and his character is revealed even more at the end of the parable. God actively seeks to find and restore those who are separated from him; he takes the initiative to reconcile them to him.

The combination of the three stories Jesus told as part of this parable forced his listeners to make a paradigm shift concerning their view of God.

Questions Raised by this Parable

Here are a few of the many questions raised by this parable:

- Exactly what did the younger son do that justified being rewarded and treated like a king upon his return?
- What is the significance of the robe? The ring? The sandals? The feast?
- Why did the older brother become angry? He, too, had received his inheritance as the same time as his brother.
- How did he know what his sibling had – or had not – done on his journey?

- How was the boy "lost"? And, who found him?

- How was the younger brother "dead" (since he showed upon the father's doorstep?) And, how and when did he come back to life again?

- Why would the father have acted in such a counter-cultural manner? (It was very strange and unusual behavior on the part of the father.)

These, and many other counter-cultural issues need to be explained by any interpreter of this parable.

Surprising Counter-Cultural Behaviors

One of the glaring "surprise twists" in this parable is the number of counter-cultural behaviors Jesus includes. They certainly are not merely coincidental, but are, most assuredly, planned and integral to his message. Many of these were such radical departures from the cultural norms that the audience would have been shocked, offended and/or angered by the behaviors demonstrated by these characters, but they served an important purpose — they modeled the types of personal transformations and psychological transitions Jesus' audience would need to accomplish in their own lives.

The main characters start out as "losers" (who are held responsible for their losses) who transform into rejoicing "seekers". They demonstrate very counter-cultural behaviors as they change and develop during their individual stories.

Younger Son's Counter-Cultural Actions

The younger son's counter-cultural behaviors included:

- Making the request for his inheritance.
- Traveling to a Gentile country.
- Feeding pigs.

- Expensive living.
- Returning home to face kezazah.
- Accepting being found.

The younger son's counter-cultural actions helped people make the shift from the old patriarchal inheritance rules to adoption, from legalistic repentance and forgiveness to grace and love, from patriarchal power, authority and dominance to freedom-giving and from rule-based obedience to loving submission – even at great risk both to the one seeking adventure and the one permitting the freedom.

Father's Counter-Cultural Actions & Attitudes

The father demonstrated a number of counter-cultural behaviors in the third story; the audience would have been beside themselves by the end of the story:

- He agreed to his son's request for premature distribution of the estate.
- According to patriarchal culture, he was essentially violating his fiduciary responsibility to the family to maintain (and, if possible, increase) the family's wealth and social standing, but by this action, he did just the opposite.
- He acted more like a mother than a father when he ran and greeted his son with obvious displays of affection – a rebellious son, who could have received the death penalty for his "rebellious" behavior.
- Then, he took younger son home and rewarded him with a robe, a ring and sandals – all signs of acceptance, forgiveness, reconciliation, and familial authority. He treated his son like an honored guest instead of a son returning empty-handed after having lost all his money.

- He overlooked the anger and rebellious behavior of the elder son who by refusing to accept father's invitation, was in effect, rejecting him and his brother, and shaming his father in the process.

The father's counter-cultural actions helped people make the shift from legalism and the law to love and grace, from patriarchal inheritance rules to adoption into the kingdom of God, from being controlling and making all the decision for the family to being a freedom-giver, and accepting the risks that go along with freedom, from demanding rights and respect to showing compassion and grace.

Elder Son's Counter-Cultural Behaviors

The elder son's counter-cultural behaviors demonstrate what can happen when small issues are not resolved and anger is allowed to simmer until it explodes. The resulting rebelliousness and emotional distancing can destroy a family. The elder son displayed counter-cultural behaviors, but for the most part, his were acts of omission rather than commission – at least up until the latter part of the story when he became aggressive and vocal with his anger:

- At the very beginning of the story, he should have stepped in as a mediator between his father and his brother (that was one of the responsibilities of an elder son), but he didn't … he remained silent … somewhere. (Maybe he was still out in the fields, which raises the question why he was never in the same place as his father?)
- He should also have refused to agree to the distribution if he was as upset about it as he appeared to be.
- When his brother returned, he should have been hospitable to his brother and offered him food and drink, as the custom required, but again, he didn't.

- In fact, he wouldn't even speak to his brother or acknowledge his return.

- He had a responsibility to help his father with hosting duties at the party, which he refused to do.

- When his father invited him to join the celebration (probably more of an "order" than a true invitation), again, he refused. His refusal was really a rejection of both his father and his brother.

At this point, his actions became more vocal and aggressive:

- When he learned that his brother had returned, he became angry and refused to go into the party.

- When his father came out and pleaded with him to join the family, he got angry with his father and he distanced himself from his brother, "this son of yours".

- Then, he accused his brother of having squandered his money "with prostitutes" – but, of course, he would have had no way of knowing what his brother did, or didn't do, on his journey in a "distant" country.

- Then, he just fades off … we hear nothing further from him.

CHAPTER 6

INTERPRETATION APPROACH

There are many interpretations of this material, and they differ considerably from one another; some directly contradict. Bailey has identified a "theological cluster" of themes related to this parable: atonement, Christology, Eschatology, Eucharist, failed leadership, family/community, fatherhood, freely offered grace, freedom, grace, the individual and the community, joy, sin, sonship, and repentance. There's no way to address all of those themes in a single volume, so the problem remains – which ones to address and which ones to ignore.

We'll be developing an interpretation here, but we do so merely to set the stage for discussion of the psychological and theological development issues presented in this parable and the lessons we can learn about God-orchestrated wilderness experiences.

In other words, for us, the interpretation is simply a vehicle to get to these other topics; it is a means to an end, not an end in itself. Consequently, this book will take a somewhat different approach; rather than trying to identify the key theme(s), it will focus on the transformation processes identified in the parable, using the four main characters' transformations as a model for believers during our own wilderness experiences.

With that caveat in mind, how should we proceed to develop our interpretation of this parable? First of all, an acceptable interpretation should address the entirety of the parable, not just one part of it. Secondly, the interpretation should be responsive to the initial criticism / question levied by the Pharisees at the beginning of the parable. And, finally, it should provide a logical, cohesive explanation of the (counter-cultural) events that are depicted in the parable, and especially in our case, the ending of the parable.

With those preliminary requirements in mind, this book will use the following additional guidelines to develop an interpretation of this parable:

- Context is critical.
- Exegesis, not isogesis.
- Scripture interprets Scripture.
- This parable reflects psychological, theological and spiritual development processes.

The following will further clarify our approach.

Context Is Critical

One of the ways we can make sure our interpretation is true to Jesus' intent is to start our interpretation looking first at the big picture, the historical-cultural setting. We want to see the entire elephant, not just the legs, the ears or the trunk. Bailey has also provided us with a key rule for interpretation:

> *"The only theological content that should be considered valid in a parable is that which the original storyteller could have intended and was available to the original audience.*
>
> *You must do your best to enter the world of the storyteller."*

Exegesis, Not Isogesis

When I first started doing my research I was astonished by the number of teachers and other commentators who made unsupported claims and leapt to unwarranted conclusions. They based their interpretations on words that weren't even in the text, or they seemed always to choose the most negative of any possible definitions of key words and symbols in the parable. They didn't even follow Jesus' clear instruction at the beginning of the chapter that his response included three stories, not just one. Their own personal biases seemed to creep in without even acknowledging their bias up-front. Their interpretations were all over the map, many contradicting one another.

As I started working on this book, I was reminded of a class I took in college - an art appreciation class. I remember that, as one of our early assignments, we were given a fish and asked to describe the fish, which we all did in about thirty seconds flat.

Our instructor, however, was singularly unimpressed with our findings. He asked us to return to the fish and describe what we saw. So, being the *"compliant"* college students that we were, we all did as requested ... spending maybe another minute or two looking at the fish ... adding our new insights to our previous list describing the fish ... and, feeling rather proud of ourselves in the process.

However, yet again, the instructor was not impressed. He had the audacity to ask us to return to the fish a third time! This time, we were to *"really look and see"* the fish and then describe what we saw. Well, as you can guess, about this time we students were getting pretty frustrated, figuring that there was nothing more that we could see - or learn - about the fish before us. Despite our visible (and verbal) frustration, the instructor kept asking us to return to the fish ... and you know what?

Every time we went back to look at the fish, we saw more details.

The fish had not changed.

Our eyes had not changed.

Yet, *our understanding had matured a great deal as we became more observant and attentive to the details before_us ... to the subtle shadings of* color or texture, to the size and shape of the various body parts, to the myriad of details that previously been *"invisible"* to us. These details had always been there - right in front of our eyes - but we simply had not seen them because we weren't looking closely enough, and we weren't paying careful attention.

The more I studied, the more I saw and the more I learned.

I hadn't thought about that art appreciation exercise for years; yet, as I write this, it seems extremely relevant to the study of this parable. Just as the teacher in my Art Appreciation class asked all of his students to proceed with an open mind and to look ... *really look and see* ... I ask you to do the same thing as you study this parable of Jesus together.

Keep Looking at the "Fish".

That's what I urge all of you to do as you read this book – or any book; as you listen to your preacher on Sunday morning, or any Christian minister on TV or in person. Learn to ask questions, do your homework, and don't let someone else's ideas or interpretations dictate your thoughts and understanding. Let the Holy Spirit be your guide, not someone with a famous name or a lot of letters behind his (or her) name.

One Point, or Multiple Points?

One of the big debates over the past century, which has caused much confusion, has been whether a parable can have more than one point, or only one? Julicher argued that a parable could have only one single point. He based his argument on the Aristotelian Greek idea of a parable as pure comparison; however, the conceptual background for the New Testament parable was not Aristotelian Greek, but Semitic.

For much of the twentieth century Julicher's argument won the day. Those who followed him ended up over-simplifying Jesus' parables by ignoring the embedded complexities. This attempt to reduce Jesus' parables to a single point has probably been the single biggest cause of the plethora of over-simplistic interpretations that exist.

This is a complex parable, and simplistic interpretations just don't work. Thankfully, Julicher's position has been superseded by a more realistic view that allows for multiple levels and multiple points, depending upon the complexity of the parable.

Since our parable is very well known and so much has been written about it, you'd expect that the many interpretations would basically all agree – at least on the major points - *but you'd be wrong*.

Avoid the Blind Men and the Elephant Syndrome

As I surveyed the various commentaries, and other analyses of this parable, I felt like I was listening to a group of blind men trying to describe an elephant. One of them had obviously found the elephant's leg, and consequently, described the elephant as short and round like a tree stump. Another blind man had clearly found the elephant's tail, since he described the elephant as being about 1-1.5 meters long, like a rope. A third blind man found the ears and described the elephant as wide, thin and wavy like a sheet in the wind.

Now, I ask you: *which man had described the "elephant"?*

None of them had described the elephant! A *leg* is not an elephant, an *ear* is not an elephant, and a *tail* is not the elephant.

Only an elephant (the whole creature) is an elephant!

When commentators start to "chunk" this parable into "pieces and parts," they run into trouble. It seems like there are as many different interpretations as there are analysts – and they differ widely, on some very significant points, for example:

- What is the scope of the parable – one story or all three?
- Who is the main character? The father? The younger son? Both sons? The elder son? Jesus? The Pharisees? Israel?
- What is the basic theme? Sin? Repentance? Reconciliation? Grace? Compassion?

- Who sinned in this parable? The Pharisees? The younger son? The elder son? The father? Everyone?

- What was the sin in the parable? Was it the younger son requesting his inheritance? Or maybe, it was the father granting the premature inheritance in the first place? Or, perhaps, it the elder son's rejection of both his brother and his father?

- Is it appropriate to use the existing patriarchal culture and its norms to explain this parable? After all, Jesus spent a lot of time challenging those cultural rules and behavioral norms.

It seems that "chunking" this parable into "pieces and parts" has only led to confusion. That, coupled with Julicher's over-simplification rule, has led to many significantly different interpretations, which frequently contradict one another.

Exegetes must do their homework "in depth" and stick with what the text actually says, without contaminating the text with their own preconceived ideas. (While it's impossible to do this completely, one should attempt to be as objective and unbiased as possible, and where presuppositions exist, they should at least be clearly identified.)

Scripture Interprets Scripture

The Bible never presents any key doctrine in a single, obscure or ambiguous way. It presents that same, key doctrine in multiple places and multiple ways. In order to develop our interpretation, we'll look at the big picture first, and then we'll do a deep dive into the details. (When I do jigsaw puzzles, I always like to see the picture on the box before I start trying to put the pieces together.)

Jesus Gave Us a Model for Interpreting His Parables

People make a lot of arguments about the best way to interpret one of Jesus' parables, but I apply Occam's razor here. If there's a simple answer, take that one. And, yes, there is a simple answer: since Jesus modeled for us how to interpret his parables; let's use it. Jesus told his disciples the "Parable of the Sower" (Matt. 13:1-9), and then he proceeded to explain to them what it meant.

When his disciples asked why he spoke in parables he told them that the message was meant for them but not for everyone; it was hidden from some. Then, Jesus then gave a very detailed explanation of the symbols in this parable (minor formatting, mine).

> *Listen then to what the parable of the sower means:*
>
> *[19] When anyone hears the message about the kingdom and does not understand it, the evil one comes and snatches away what was sown in their heart. This is the seed sown along the path.*
>
> *[20] The seed falling on rocky ground refers to someone who hears the word and at once receives it with joy. [21] But since they have no root, they last only a short time. When trouble or persecution comes because of the word, they quickly fall away.*
>
> *[22] The seed falling among the thorns refers to someone who hears the word, but the worries of this life and the deceitfulness of wealth choke the word, making it unfruitful.*
>
> *[23] But the seed falling on good soil refers to someone who hears the word and understands it. This is the one who produces a crop, yielding a hundred, sixty or thirty times what was sown.*

In the "Parable of the Weeds," which followed the "Parable of the Sower," Jesus explicitly identified the kingdom of God as being the spiritual referent to one of his concrete images:

> *Jesus told them another parable: "The kingdom of heaven is like a man who sowed good seed in his field. (Matt 13:14)*

When the disciples asked Jesus to explain this parable, he identified the Son of Man as the one who sowed the good seed and the good seed stood for the people of the kingdom. He said that the weeds are the people of the evil one, and the enemy who sows them is the devil.

Four Potential Levels of Meaning

Clearly his parables included multiple levels and included theological themes. By his explanation, you know that he never intended his simple, concrete images to stand on their own; they represented something else – a higher spiritual reality, generally relating to the kingdom of God, or his role as Messiah.

Today's prevailing school of thought allows for a parable to have multiple levels of meaning. Bailey argues that Jesus' parables have as many as four levels.

Superficial Story

The first level delivers a superficial story that anyone, even a child, could understand. Although Jesus' parables were true at this basic level, he didn't come to teach farmers how to grow better crops or fathers how to be better parents. The superficial story isn't the core message.

Ethical Message

The second level frequently delivered an ethical message, and the Pharisees (being the ethicists that they were) would have readily picked up on that level. We see this clearly in the story of the shepherd who had lost one of his sheep. The Pharisees would never have lowered themselves to being a shepherd, but they understood the absolute necessity of the shepherd going in search of the sheep. The shepherd would not have been able to return to his village until he had either found the sheep itself, or had some evidence that an animal had killed it.

Theological Message

The third level spoke to theology, and it is at this level that Jesus spoke about the kingdom of God. This level was difficult for most people to grasp because it was so new, different, and it departed drastically from cultural norms. Even his disciples, who had traveled with him for three years, had difficulty understanding the kingdom of God message.

Christological Message

The fourth level, when present, delivered some truth about Jesus himself. Our parable speaks a great deal about Jesus because that was the Pharisees' primary interest. They wanted to know what motivated him to associate with sinners and unclean people. They wanted to know why he ignored their rules about the Sabbath and their purity rules about eating. They wanted to know why he allowed himself to become a sinner in their eyes by ignoring these rules.

Do Your Own Study and Due-Diligence

It would be nice if we could just walk uncritically in the footsteps of those who've gone before, but to do so, would get us into trouble. If you uncritically accept someone else's interpretation, it's easy to be misled. We need to personally do the homework necessary to validate their conclusions – and either make them your own, or reject them.

That reminds me of winters where I grew up in Illinois. Occasionally when driving down the highway, I'd get stuck in the middle of a very bad snowstorm, a blizzard. The driving snow would come so hard and so fast that it was difficult to see the road, stay in my lane, and keep out of the ditch. Sometimes, I would come upon a big eighteen wheeler with lots of lights ablaze. It was convenient to just tuck in behind him and follow those lights down the road – they were much easier to see than the lane markers. However, I was putting myself at risk to do so – what guarantee did I have that he could see the road any better than I could?

In fact, it was probable that his visibility was just as limited as mine. So, why did I feel safer and more confident following along in his wake?

I was actually just deceiving myself, and abdicating responsibility for my own life-and-death decisions.

What Jesus Might Have Intended

Jesus Intended His Mission and His Role

With respect to what Jesus could possibly have intended – that's wide open considering he is God and knows all; however, he explained to his followers on numerous occasions why he came, and what his mission involved, so that seems like a good starting point.

His message was so radical and revolutionary, that it created "disruptive change" everywhere he went. Disruptive changes create a "Neutral Zone," which is that time-space between having left the old situation, but prior to reaching the new situation and establishing new norms and guidelines for daily living.

Life can become quite confusing and overwhelming in the "Neutral Zone" until the new operating rules are firmly established and commonly accepted. Consider some of the components of Jesus' radical and revolutionary message. He:

- Brought division, not peace.
- Replaced the Old Covenant with the New Covenant and the kingdom of God.
- Challenged the Shame/Honor value system.
- Confronted Messianic Expectations.
- Claimed to be God.
- Challenged patriarchy.
- Introduced the kingdom family.
- Elevated the low status of women.

- Challenged adultery and divorce laws.
- Replaced inheritance with adoption.
- Offered people a new identity.
- Confronted legalism and hypocrisy.

Think of it like an "8.0 Cultural Earthquake" – something that shook the world, toppled conventions, destroyed legalism and hypocrisy, and enabled the introduction of the kingdom of God. He introduced an entirely new world order that it would take the people some time to become comfortable in that new world.

Considering the above list, what about patriarchy did he not challenge? It clearly points out that Jesus was not a fan of patriarchy.

*Therefore, patriarchy should **not** be used as the framework for explaining his intention with this parable.*

Disruptive Changes Require Transitions

Adjusting to disruptive change is difficult; it requires a lot of internal psychological processing. Disruptive change is much more involved that just situational change.

For example, assume you just bought a new house in your same city and plan to move in right away. This is situational change, and while the actual work involved in making the move happen can be very tiring, the required emotional and psychological processing is minimal.

Now assume that instead of buying a house in your own city, you and your family are going to move to China for a couple of years because your spouse just got a big promotion at work. Now, you'll have to deal with a new job (maybe a new company), a different culture, a different language, a different monetary system, and a host of other things that will only become apparent during your stay. You'll need to make a number or paradigm shifts in order to operate effectively in this new environment.

This is disruptive change and it requires a much bigger emotional investment in being able to assimilate the change. Completing this emotional and psychological change is what is known as making the transition. When you first arrive in China, chances are very good that you will feel overwhelmed, confused, scared, and probably pretty exhausted as well. But by the end of your two-year tour; however, you'll probably feel very comfortable with the language and the customs, the money ... pretty much everything about your new home. When you start to feel comfortable in the new situation, you'll know you have completed the required psychological and emotional transition.

Jesus' Audience Needed to Make Transitions

In order for the Jews to grasp Jesus' message, they were in a similar situation to my hypothetical relocation to China. All the old operating rules were gone; they needed to make a number of paradigm shifts to adapt to those disruptive changes, including shifts:

- From patriarchy to the kingdom of God.
- From inheritance to adoption.
- From women as property to women as daughters of the kingdom.
- From external behaviors to attitudes of the heart.
- From obedient submission to loving choice.
- From shame vs. honor to servanthood.
- From Messiah as conquering hero to Messiah as suffering servant.
- From God the Father to the triune God.

This new reality required people to re-evaluate their beliefs and come to a decision as to who Jesus really was. People had to choose, no "fence-sitting" allowed. If they chose to follow Jesus and accept his worldview, that choice required them to make a number of paradigm shifts regarding their own worldview and some significant action steps to implement his commandments, some of which had a high social cost associated with them.

Jesus' Parables Spoke to His Mission

Parables are central to Jesus' ministry. We're fortunate in that Jesus very clearly told us what his mission was and why he came. Jesus described his mission saying that:

1) He *"must preach the good news of the kingdom of God"* (Luke 4:43), and that

2) *"The Son of Man came to seek and to save the lost"* (Luke 19:10).

His Mission Was to Preach the Kingdom of God

Jesus told his parables specifically to introduce and explain the kingdom of God and his role as Messiah. As he stood in front of them, Jesus said, *"the kingdom of God is in your midst"* (Luke 17:21b). This concept of the "kingdom of God" was the central, organizing principle regarding his ministry. It is repeated many times throughout the Gospels (and in later writings of Paul, and even in Revelation). As historian Michael Grant stated, everything Jesus did centered around the kingdom of God:

> *every thought and saying of Jesus was directed and subordinated to one single thing ..., the realization of the Kingdom of God upon the earth, this one phrase [Kingdom of God] sums up his whole ministry and his whole life's work*

The following eight parables explicitly address the kingdom of god. Chronologically, these kingdom of God parables were told in this order (*prior to the story of the shepherd who had lost his sheep, which was the 29th*).

- #12 – Weeds among good plants (Kingdom of Heaven) (Matthew 13:24-30, 36-43)
- #13 – Growing seed (Kingdom of Heaven) (Mark 4:26-29)

- #14 – Mustard seed (Kingdom of Heaven) (Matthew 13:31-32; Mark 4:30-32; Luke 13:18-19)
- #15 – Yeast (Kingdom of Heaven) (Matt 13:33; Luke 13:20-21)
- #16 – Hidden treasure (Kingdom of Heaven) (Matthew 13:44)
- #17 – Valuable pearl (Kingdom of Heaven) (Matthew 13:45-46)
- #18 – Fishing net (Kingdom of Heaven) (Matthew 13:47-50)
- #19 – Owner of a house (Kingdom of Heaven) (Matthew 13:52)

A New Covenant, a New Kingdom and a New Reality

Jesus brought a new reality with a New Covenant, the kingdom of God and a radically different Messiah from the one the Jews were expecting. These were all disruptive changes. The Jewish people needed to change their vision of reality to match Jesus' mission and role.

The Parables Spoke to His Person

Jesus portrayed himself in many different ways in his parables: the sower, the judge in the end-times, the rock, the shepherd, the bridegroom, the father, the giver of forgiveness, the vineyard owner, the lord. In this way, he made an implicit claim to be God. In fact, the arguments he used depended upon the hearer making the association between himself and God.

Jesus' approach to parables was unique; none of the prophets used parables in the same way. None of them applied God symbols to themselves nor did they claim they were doing the things that only God would do.

Jesus used parables to accomplish many purposes, but one of the important purposes was to fulfill prophecy. There are more than one hundred prophecies that speak to Jesus' fulfilling the role of the Messiah, but did you realize that prophecy *foretold that he would speak in parables*? Matthew 13:34-35 tells you:

Jesus spoke all these things to the crowd in parables; he did not say anything to them without using a parable.

So was fulfilled what was spoken through the prophet:

"I will open my mouth in parables,

I will utter things hidden since the creation of the world."

By using parables, Jesus was actually fulfilling prophecy as recorded in Psalms 78:2. Clearly, parables were an important tool for Jesus.

Use the Kingdom of God to Explain the Parable

Given the significant ways Jesus challenged patriarchy and the religious leaders of the day, he was not a supporter of patriarchy and would not use it to explain his intention as he preached about the New Covenant and the kingdom of God. While both patriarchy and the prevailing culture are appropriate tools to explain how Jesus' **audience** may have reacted to this story, they are **not appropriate** to explain **what Jesus intended** by this story.

Several of the characters in this parable demonstrate shockingly counter-cultural behaviors; ones that would have caught Jesus' audience totally by surprise, offended them, and made them angry. Many of his audience would have called these behaviors "sin."

According to the cultural perspective,

- The father betrayed his role as steward of the family fortunes – so why did he agree to the distribution?
- Rebellion in a child was grounds for the death sentence, so why did the father welcome him back and elevate his status rather than kill him?
- The elder son should have received a double portion of the inheritance – and the major blessing – so what is wrong with the elder son's attitude?

- Promiscuity struck at the very heart of patriarchy – it could have compromised the blood lines and muddied up the inheritance rights
- Polygamy was common – where was the mother in the story?
- It was considered a sin to fail to share food with those in need – so how could the elder son (legalist that he was), fail in his "duty"?
- Failure to be hospitable was equivalent to rejection – why would the elder son reject his father's invitation (i.e., his master's "command")?
- Sharing a meal indicated reconciliation, peaceful relations and assurance that there was no loss of relationship – why would the father overlook the "rebellion" of his son?
- Normally, a host would repeat his invitation until it was accepted – so why didn't the father persist with the elder son?

Clearly, Jesus challenged the cultures' definition of sin, salvation, righteousness, and even God. Jesus did not support patriarchy or the prevailing culture in a number of areas. He challenged many of the cultural foundations. He was introducing something completely new.

Trying to use the old to explain the new just won't work. It is not appropriate to use the very things that Jesus criticized as the basis for explaining his intentions in this parable. An appropriate interpretation of this parable must explain how these counter-cultural behaviors support Jesus' message, rather than detract from his message, and also, how the characters can have two different personas in the same story.

Throughout the Gospels, there are many examples demonstrating that Jesus' values were different from those around him. For example, he and the Father both valued extravagant generosity (PS. 36:5-8):

- God's gift of free will was expensive and extravagant.
- Jesus' taking the form of a human being and coming to earth was extravagant.

- His death on the cross was exceedingly expensive and extravagant on God's part.

God's love is extravagant, expensive and totally unwarranted by any goodness your part.

In the New Testament accounts, you see Jesus not only accepting but affirming acts that many would consider wasteful. In many cases the things Jesus did or commended were considered extravagant, or even wasteful, by many especially the Pharisees, but did their objections make it so?

On at least two occasions women poured expensive oil or perfume on Jesus' feet, and while those around them complained that it was wasteful, Jesus commended the women's actions (Matt. 26:8; Luke 7:44–47). He even went so far as to forgive one of the women's sins because of her actions.

When Jesus' disciples asked him how many times they needed to forgive someone, he told them "70 x 7" which most of you think means 490 times … which is a lot, but that really wasn't what Jesus meant. That phrase has an Old Testament referent – Lamech, son of Cain, who was a murderer worse than his father but sought vengeance on his enemies far above the degree of damage they had done to him (Gen. 23-24). Jesus was telling his disciples that they should forgive far and above the need for the forgiveness; they should forgive excessively, extravagantly.

Is God's extravagantly generous love wasteful? God doesn't think so.

Why Use Symbols?

Why would Jesus disguise his important message in symbols rather than clear language? Wouldn't he want to make his message obvious so that everyone would "get it". When Jesus told his disciples the "Parable of the Sower" (Matthew 13:1-30), they asked him why he spoke in parables. He explained, very clearly, that the message was given to some, but not all.

In this passage, you see themes of election and God's sovereignty. The "Parable of the Sower" was the 11th parable Jesus told. By the time Jesus got around to telling our parable, his followers had heard his core message repeated many times through a variety of parables. Like any good teacher, Jesus used repetition as one of his key communication tools.

He told them he used parables in fulfillment of prophecy and to demonstrate his sovereignty. Some would hear and understand, and others would be prevented from hearing and understanding.

The genre allowed Jesus to communicate these secrets to his followers (who shared his mental model) while, at the same time, hiding that information from his opponents. Since his opponents didn't share his mental model, they didn't have the "key" to decode his message.

Any interpretation that doesn't recognize the eschatological implications of this parable has missed Jesus' primary point.

Jesus Counter-Cultural Messages Helped People Make Paradigm Shifts

Jesus used the counter-cultural behaviors in this parable help people redefine their conception of God and the new kingdom rules and operational guidelines. The parabolic genre helped people visualize the kingdom of God, and how it would look and feel. The parable helped Jesus' audience begin to make the necessary psychological and emotional transitions to assimilate properly into the kingdom of God world.

What Would Jesus' Audience Have Known?
Their Historical-Cultural Context

After having spent centuries under foreign domination, and constantly having to protect their religious beliefs from foreigners, Jesus' audience would have been very familiar with their national and cultural history. His audience should have been familiar with all of the following:

- The entire sweep of Jewish history, including the Exodus, foreign domination, Hellenism, etc.
- The competing mixture of social, religious, political and cultural perspectives in first century Israel
- Strong knowledge Hebrew Scriptures, including the Septuagint
- The common symbols and their spiritual referents
- Jesus' Prior Teachings – he told twenty-eight parables before this one in Luke 15

References to the Old Testament

The Pharisees were experts in the Hebrew law, and they would immediately have recognized and understood any Old Testament references, especially any from the book of Exodus (considering Exodus told the story of the Jews had wandering in the desert for forty years).

When it came to the story of the man with two sons, the Pharisees being very knowledgeable of the Scripture would immediately have remembered the many stories of sibling rivalry in the Old Testament, for example: Cain and Abel, Jacob and Esau, Joseph and his brothers. They would also have recognized the typical pattern. Theologian James Jordan observed: *"When the older brother apostatizes, and is judged, the younger brother replaces him."* They would also have recognized that when Israel was divided into two kingdoms, Israel was considered the elder, while Judah was considered the younger.

Prior Parables

Knowledge of the Kingdom of God

Jesus' ministry had grown from a small group of disciples to a large crowd of "followers," who traveled with him, and followed him from town to town (Luke 7:11, 14:25). During the course of his public ministry, Jesus taught many truths using parables. Since his followers were with him day-in and day-out, they would have heard those truths repeated in many different ways as they traveled with him. Specifically, they would have been familiar with the prior twenty-eight parables that Jesus told before this Luke 15 parable.

While his kingdom of God message was certainly new, revolutionary and counter-cultural to the larger Jewish population, it was not new to his followers. They had already heard him preach at least eight parables that explicitly dealt with the kingdom of God, and many others that implicitly addressed the same topic as they traveled with him.

Jesus Called People to Transformation

An important part of Jesus' kingdom of God message was his call to a new identity. He invited people to become part of the family of God by way of adoption. The goal was spiritual maturity and transformation:

> Do not conform to the pattern of this world, but be transformed by the renewing of your mind. Then you will be able to test and approve what God's will is—his good, pleasing and perfect will. (Rom. 12:2)

We Will Focus On Transformation

Many possible themes have been identified as relating to this parable, and many interpreters have struggled to determine which one(s) should be primary and which one(s) should be ignored. Given the complexity of this parable, that is a daunting task.

Rather than trying to pick one (or more) of these themes to focus on, this book will approach the parable from a different angle. It will focus on the transformations of the main characters in the three stories, and use them to extrapolate a general process by which God acts to bring about spiritual growth and maturity among believers. We'll use Bonhoeffer's critical needs list, the Relational Life Tasks Model, the Paradigm of Personhood, and Attachment Theory as the basis for the following discussion.

Bonhoeffer identified the following needs for coming to terms with the ambiguities of human existence:

the need for affirmation, for belonging, for restoration and healing, for being a significant person, and for not being forgotten.

These human needs drive the individual directly to God as the source of personhood.

The Relational Life Tasks model includes the following psychological tasks to be mastered: 1) Identity (gaining self), 2) Integrity (saving/completing self), 3) Intimacy (sharing self) and 4) Industry (investing self).

Anderson's Paradigm of Personhood describes the theological development process for becoming a person: 1) Election (God's sovereign choice) as the affirmation of the self, 2) Covenant (binding agreement between God and humanity), including the relatedness of the self, 3) Salvation/atonement as the healing of the self, and 4) Eschaton (the final goal) as the significance of the self.

The psychological and theological processes are intimately related as follows:

- Identity relates to Election.
- Intimacy relates to Covenant.
- Integrity relates to Salvation/Atonement.
- Industry relates to Eschaton.

CHAPTER 7

TRANSFORMATION HAPPENS IN THE WILDERNESS

God Orchestrates Wilderness Journeys

God Will Use Family, Social, Political Conflicts

God orchestrates wilderness journeys, and he'll use any means necessary to get you there – even things like family stress and conflict (as in our parable). He wants to remove the distractions from our lives so that we can focus on strengthening our relationship with him. God leads believers into the desert so he can develop a closer, more intimate relationship and meet their needs for significance and security.

And, yes, I did say God puts you into that wilderness experience. Just like he did with Jesus when the Holy Spirit led him into the wilderness – and why? So that he could be tempted by the devil. That doesn't sound right, does it? But that's what the Bible says happened.

God Removes Distractions

As part of this wilderness experience, God calls you to leave your old life behind, and in doing so, he frequently removes a lot of the "toys" that you've come to enjoy (perhaps too much!). God is a jealous God, and he doesn't want your affections being diverted to any other person or thing. He wants you to love him for who he is, not for the "toys" that he gives you, and the only way he can do that is to (temporarily, at least) take them away from you.

God Doesn't Think of Time the Way You Do

God is willing to invest a lot of time in you because he loves you and wants to see you become the person you were predestined to be. He's willing to spend as much time as it takes to prepare his people to fulfill their destinies. He was willing to have Moses and the Israelites spend 40 years in the wilderness because of their disobedience (even though the physical distance could have been crossed in a few short weeks).

John the Baptist spent 30 years in the wilderness preparing for his six-month ministry to introduce Jesus to the world. John had a big job to do, and God knew that would take a lot of time to prepare. God didn't consider that lengthy time period unnecessary or overkill, but a prudent way to protect John from outside influences and give him the attention he deserved for his ministry.

God thinks in terms of eternity, not just the here and now, so what might seem like a waste of time (or, overkill) to you, is critically important in God's overall plan.

God Wants an Intimate Relationship With You

Most people would prefer to avoid the "Wilderness Experience," but unfortunately, God calls his followers to the desert at some point in their lives. Your time in the desert is all about transformation. God uses that time and space to refine you and help you realize your true identity.

He wants you to give up self-control, and depend upon him alone. He wants to refine you so that you become the person you were created to be. As you experience the tests, temptations and challenges the wilderness brings, you can forge a binding agreement with God that includes the relatedness of self, a covenant relationship. You can develop a secure attachment to him, and rest in him, knowing that you are secure and he will never leave you or abandon you.

Characteristics of the Wilderness Experience

Attention Getting

All of a sudden, you find yourself engulfed in some major crisis; perhaps you've had to file bankruptcy, your home and all your possessions (including all those irreplaceable wedding and baby pictures!) were destroyed in a massive California wild fire, or you've just been diagnosed with some serious medical condition. Whatever the particulars, God has your attention, and he is now in the process of transforming you.

Customized Just for You!

Each person's wilderness journey will be somewhat different, since God "customizes" the experience for each one of us, but wilderness journeys tend to have some common elements: you didn't choose them, they tend to be difficult and painful, you don't know where you're going or how to get there, and you probably feel totally lost while you're in the wilderness.

Leave the Past Behind

Wilderness experiences require you to leave your past behind, with all its responsibilities and social safety nets behind (at least for a time) and move off into some (possibly) isolated, barren, uninhabited place so that you can get some uninterrupted, quality time with God. The wilderness experience is designed for you to get to know God better, and making sacrifices is an important step in that direction.

Lose Your Excess Baggage

The wilderness has a way of stripping off everything that is external, temporary and worthless, leaving only the essence (or "substance") behind. Taylor observes:

In the wilderness, everything becomes 110 percent what it is. Without all the usual background noise and distraction, there is nothing to dilute reality. All of the ordinary filters do not work.

The key point here is that people in the midst of a wilderness experience become an even purer, clearer, "cleaner" version of their true selves; their real identities show through.

Roller-Coaster Emotions

Separation (from family, friends or other important figures in your lives) tends to leave you with feelings of loss, sadness, and grief. Sometimes you feel angry with the people who are no longer present in your life (many children have felt angry with a parent who has died suddenly). Sometimes you'll be angry with God – for much the same reasons the child gets angry with the missing parent. Or, perhaps you start feeling hopeless or depressed or doubtful or scared …

Disruptive Change

Disruptive change forces you to leave your previous life behind and enter into some unknown, undesired, and challenging existence, for who knows how long. You have no maps or GPS's to guide you on your journey. All you have is your faith in God and his Word to guide you (and, fortunately for you, that's enough!).

You may find yourself in the middle of a crisis that totally rocks your world. Everything you've come to rely upon to provide security and stability is suddenly gone: you may be facing the loss of a much-needed job, the long-tem illness of a close family member, or perhaps, your marriage is being torn apart.

Not only do such changes cause problems, but they frequently knock your support systems out from under you as well. The old rules of what to do and how to behave all fly out the window, but there are no new rules to take their place.

Your problems may seem so big that you feel your very survival is at stake.

Neutral Zone

The wilderness is also known as the "Neutral Zone." It's a place that is "betwixt and between;" it is like standing on the threshold of a room – you are neither in the room, nor out of the room.

It's the time and space where you've left your old life, as well as the rules and infrastructure that governed your daily life, behind but since you haven't yet emerged from the wilderness, you haven't developed the new rules and procedures that correspond to your new identity. (I liken the neutral zone to a flying trapeze artist who's just released the swing he was holding and is now flying through the air. At this moment, he has nothing to support him and is depending solely upon his momentum – and the guy on the other swing to catch him.) It is in this kind of "limbo land" where God refines you and reveals your "true self" - the person you were meant to be.

It is a time of God-orchestrated testing, but it may also be a time of intensified temptation and spiritual attack. You need to rely upon God's Word especially at times like these; your feelings and emotions are not likely to be helpful guides; they may actually make you more susceptible to Satan's attacks.

The wilderness experience (or neutral zone) can be a frightening, and sometimes, overwhelming place – but at least it's temporary!

Single Ticket

Perhaps one of the hardest things about the desert experience is that you have to travel through it by yourself. No one else can experience it the same way you will; they don't have your genetic makeup, they haven't had the same childhood, they haven't had the same marriage or the special needs child, they didn't serve overseas in a war zone seeing things no human being should ever have to see. Consequently, no one else can truly experience or understand what you do as you traverse your wilderness.

Harsh Environments and Challenging Tests

Wilderness experiences tend to be difficult, challenging times of testing and/or temptation. Often the environment is isolated and perhaps, harsh. Sometimes they are physically harsh as in the Judean desert Moses and the Israelites faced (where simply finding food and water is a major challenge), but more often they are emotionally harsh.

There's a reason for that harsh environment; it pulls your mind away from your old life and forces you to focus on the here and now. God wants to develop a secure attachment with you. Unfortunately, suffering and stress are primary catalysts in that process.

Transformation Goals and Process

The spiritual and psychological sides of life are inextricably related and work together to produce spiritual maturity. God has called many of the heroes of the faith to enjoy a nice stroll through the desert. Why, then, should you be surprised when you find yourself stuck in the middle of the desert or wilderness with little or no idea how you got there, let alone how you're going to get out.

These psychological and theological processes are relevant to everyone's spiritual journey.

God Is Transforming You

If you're in the wilderness right now, God is transforming you. Don't try to shortcut the experience or try to get out of it altogether. God is sovereign and he has a plan. If you bail from your desert experience too soon, you'll miss out on the blessings that God has in store for you later on – blessings that will depend upon what you learned in the wilderness.

The Desert Is God's Preferred Learning Laboratory

God has used desert experiences throughout history with most of the faith heroes of the Bible, including: Moses, Elijah, Jeremiah, David, Job, John the Baptist, Peter, Paul and even, Jesus. Some of them, like Moses and David had multiple wilderness experiences! Some of them, like Moses and John the Baptist, were in the desert for decades! But, regardless of the length of time they spent in their desert or the particular tests they had to face, wilderness experiences always brought disruptive change into their lives.

Stress Is the Catalyst for Transformation

God wants to develop a secure attachment with you, and stress is typically required to trigger the attachment process. The wilderness is well suited for providing the necessary level of stress to accomplish that goal. Wilderness experiences will almost always require you to stretch your faith muscles.

When you're in the desert, it may seem that God has disappeared, but in reality, he's right there with you. He will frequently remain silent and out of sight because he doesn't want to interfere with your exercise of free will. He wants you to come out of the wilderness with a deep love for him – because of who he is, not because of the blessings he gives you. When it seems like God is far away, that just gives you an opportunity to exercise your faith muscles (Heb. 11:1).

The wilderness may seem harsh, dangerous, lonely and overwhelming, but God has a plan, and the wilderness experience is part of it.

Trade Self-Reliance for Dependence Upon God

God wants to strip you of your self-reliance, so he will frequently wait until you've given up obsessing about some desire or prayer, and then he will step in and answer it. There are many examples in the Bible where God waited a long time to answer people's prayers ... what many of you would consider "too long." But God is sovereign, and he always has a plan. His actions may not make sense to you – especially if you're knee-deep in desert sand at the time, but you need to trust in his ultimate goodness and justice.

Suffering Has a Purpose

In addition to providing the necessary catalyst for attachment, suffering has a number of other purposes / benefits:

- Suffering helps us to shift our sights from our earthly existence to heaven and our eternal future.
- Suffering (especially grief) helps us let go of the past and move forward with our lives.
- Suffering proves the authenticity of our faith
- It produces perseverance and character.
- It teaches us humility and compassion for others.
- Suffering leads us to repentance.
- Suffering teaches us to surrender self-reliance and depend upon God.
- Suffering leads to righteousness.
- Even Jesus learned obedience through suffering.
- Suffering reminds us of Jesus' sacrifice for us.

Develop Intimacy with God

God likes to work with his people in the desert because there are fewer distractions and he can more easily get your attention. Harsh environments increase your dependence on him. Your self-reliance won't be sufficient. He tells you, *"You will seek me and find me when you seek me with all your heart."* (Jer. 29:13).

Knowing God Involves a Real Relationship

When you're in the wilderness, your mind and your emotions are probably not the best guides for decision-making, and one of the lessons God is teaching you is to stop being self-reliant and become more dependent upon him. A good way to start practicing that is by getting deeper into the word of God. A byproduct of your desert experience is very likely going to be increased hunger for the Word of God, and that is a good thing.

Knowing God is a whole-being experience involving the mind, the will, and the feelings. It is an intellectual, emotional and volitional relationship, which was initiated by God. It is a real relationship involving God's personal affection, redeeming action, covenant faithfulness, and providential watchfulness.

Communion with God is a two-way street that results in glory to God. Communion assumes a positive atmosphere of love, joy and fellowship, although sometimes he may exert some divine discipline. You were created to commune with God (Is. 43:7) and glorify him in the process.

Develop Spiritual Growth

Spiritual growth is all about drawing closer to God and increasingly reflecting his attributes. You can draw closer through prayer and getting deeper into the Word. You will increasingly demonstrate integrity and Christian character, and you will persevere through trials and hardships.

And those he predestined, he also called; those he called, he also justified; those he justified, he also glorified. (Rom. 8:30)

The basic premise for the following discussion is that God is the source of personhood, and he wants to have an intimate relationship with his family of believers. In order for that to happen, believers need to become spiritually mature.

Balance and Harmony

Maturity strives for balance and harmony. Specifically, there needs to be balance among the following psychological needs: belonging and separating, realizing and expressing, contributing and caring, anchoring and acknowledging, and between imitating and devoting. Spirituality serves to anchor the self in a reality that recognizes that God is the source of your personhood as well as your purpose and meaning in life.

Industry and Eschaton

Work itself, can become a medium of loving and an expression of your mission or purpose in life – when your labor conforms to the goal of expressing care for others, when both how the work is done and what is done contribute to the realization of that basic human need to share your self with another.

Imitate God's Revelation, or Withdraw from Intimacy

God shows himself through divine revelation. That leads to a new relationship of forgiveness and acceptance. Your response to God's revelation can be to either withdrawal or reciprocity, i.e., imitation. Learning to share your self with God creates integrity and opens the door to intimacy with God. Achieving your intended purpose as a human being (integrity) is equated with expressing intimacy with God.

Intimacy and Industry Converge in the Need to Love and Work

Intimacy and industry converge in the need to love and to work. Having a solid sense of self is required before you can expect to care for others or contribute to the larger society from your unique giftedness. The goal for both spiritual and psychological development is maturity. Paul reminds us that sanctification is a lifelong process and we must persevere to the end:

> *Forgetting what is behind and straining toward what is ahead, I press on toward the goal to win the prize for which God has called me heavenward in Christ Jesus. (Phil. 3:12-14)*

Discover Your True Self

Relationship with God Anchors the Self

Spirituality functions to anchor the self in a reality that transcends self. Your sense of self is dependent on the existence of a personal God. It is through the receptivity of God that we find our true identity. We are welcomed, we receive God's attention, we meet and we allow ourselves to be met. This is where we experience true healing through meeting. Anchoring significantly affects identity issues such as self-worth, purpose and meaning in life. Through your acknowledgment of God and relationship with him, you gain self as you experience separateness and belongingness in the relationship.

Integrate Your Dark Side

Theologically and psychologically, you need to come to grips with your dark side – whether you call that side "the old man" or "the shadow," you must resolve the tension between the good and the bad we all carry within ourselves. Jung contended that a conscious integration of your shadow is essential if you are to establish human relationships.

93

Satan Will Pay an Unwanted Visit

Satan Will Try to Make You Doubt God, or Disobey Him

As you draw closer to God, Satan will begin to take notice. Satan pays attentions to what's happening in our lives and when he sees someone making great strides in their spiritual life, he feels threatened and will get in their face and try to mess up their lives somehow.

One of his favorites tactics, especially when you're in the midst of the desert experience is to plant doubts in your mind. You might suddenly discover you have a lot of thoughts like the following bouncing around in your head:

- Does God really exist?
- Why is he being silent?
- I feel like my prayers are bouncing off the ceiling.
- I really blew it this time!
- God must be angry with me.

You need to rely upon the Word of God and the armor of God at those times especially. Otherwise, the devil will use those feelings as an opening for a spiritual attack.

The desert will be tough; there's no easy way around that, and if you do find some way to exit the experience prematurely, you will only have hurt yourself. Don't fall for Satan's lies! God loves you – unconditionally – and, no, he's NOT angry with you! It may feel like he's playing hide-n-seek with you right now, but that's just so you have a chance to develop your faith and exercise your free will. Satan may try to convince you that there's some shortcut or "easy button" to get you out of this experience. Don't fall for that lie either!

Be Patient and Let God Be God

Just be patient, and let God do his work of transformation in your life. Draw your strength from him; don't try to rely upon your own strength. Dig into his Word –for your own personal growth, but also as your number one weapon against the wiles of the devil. Do what Jesus did – speak God's word to him, and he will flee from you.

God Loves You & Won't Abandon You

God loves you unconditionally and he will see you through this wilderness experience. The time of testing can be very difficult and it may feel like God has abandoned you, but he hasn't – and he won't. Some faith heroes have referred to their time in the desert as "the dark night of the soul". When you're in the desert, you tend to feel like God has forgotten you and that he is angry with you. That is clearly not the truth, but you all feel that way sometimes.

Remember, too, no matter how bad things may seem right now, *nothing* ... I repeat ... nothing can separate you from God's love, or his plan! (Rom. 8:38) God is with you throughout the entire wilderness experience, even when he is silent and seems to have disappeared. He loves you, cares for you, and protects you while you're in the wilderness.

The Characters Transformed into Seekers

Characters Grew and Developed

Jesus used a unique and unusual technique in this parable – each of the main characters had both a negative and a positive persona, and those characters changed and evolved during their respective stories. The elder son was the only character that remained relatively static (his situation seemed to deteriorate rather than grow and mature).

Characters Started as Losers

All of our main characters started out as "losers". The shepherd and the woman, like the father, had all lost something. These characters each had a responsibility and/or leadership failure. The shepherd lost a sheep, the woman lost a coin; and the father lost his son(s). The younger son has taken his inheritance, left home, and lost all his money. The elder son lost all sense of what it meant to be a son and heir to his father. In each case, the "loser" was deemed **responsible** for losing the item and held accountable for the loss.

Theological Considerations

The story also has a number of theological considerations, such as: sin, election, repentance, salvation and atonement, purpose and meaning. Several interesting questions are raised in this parable:

- What is sin?
- Who sinned?
- What is the nature of repentance?
- Why does one who was elected have to take the "long way" home?
- Do pain and suffering mean that we're on the wrong path?

Psychological Considerations

There are a number of psychological issues involved in this story: attachment, identity and intimacy issues were prominent throughout. The family seemed to be dealing with the launching phase of the family life cycle and with issues of belonging vs. separation. There appeared to be some sort of ongoing family conflict. From the beginning of the story, the three key figures appear to be estranged from one another; they didn't communicate well, and they seemed to feel distress when in one another's presence.

Identity – Answers the Question, "Who am I?"

Both sons in our parable were dealing with identity issues. Identity is all about gaining self, and answers the question *"Who am I?"* By necessity, it also answer the question *"Who am I not?"* These questions can only be answered in a relational context. Gaining self is the process of developing a solid "basic self" and includes the discovery of your physical and mental boundaries, thus enabling you to recognize that both your mind and body belong to you, i.e., your "self, " and not someone else.

Identity Requires Both Belonging and Separation

Personal identity requires two things: a sense of belonging and a sense of separateness. This parable clearly portrays that tension. Belonging and separation were major issues for both sons. All three identified family members were estranged from one another, and both of the sons were clearly feeling the tension between belonging and separating. They each chose different paths trying to reconcile those issues. The younger brother was ultimately more successful than the elder brother.

Good Personas Represent God and Jesus

In each story, Jesus used a different character to portray himself as he explained to the Pharisees why he would eat with sinners. Fortunately, they didn't stay "bad" personas very long; they transformed into their "good" personas in the wilderness. Each of these characters transformed (from his or her "bad" personas to a "good" personas) by passing through a "wilderness experience".

Characters Transform

For each of the main characters in our parable, the goal of the transformation process was to become an appropriate symbol for Jesus as he responded to the Pharisees. The following characters experienced transformation in this parable; the elder son did not.

- The "bad" shepherd became the "good" shepherd.
- The "bad" woman became the "good" woman.
- The "bad (prodigal)" son became the "good" son.
- The "bad" father became the "good" father.

The Bad Shepherd Becomes the Good Shepherd (God Symbol)

Shepherds were very common in Israel, and everyone would have been familiar with them. In addition, they were mentioned frequently in the Bible; however, their status changed considerably over the centuries.

Being a shepherd was both a difficult and dangerous job; it was pretty much a 7x24 job. In the morning the shepherd would move the sheep from the pen to the pasture. He would actively monitor them throughout the day, ensuring they had the necessary food and water, and always being on the alert for predators, or other dangers. At the end of the day, he would move the sheep back to the fold for the night, but even, then he had to remain alert for any potential dangers.

The biggest difference between a good shepherd and a bad shepherd was where he placed his focus. A good shepherd kept his focus and his attention on the sheep, their provision, guidance and safety. He ensured they had food and water. And, he led them … he didn't follow along behind. He was personally involved with his sheep; he knew his sheep and they knew his voice.

Back in the days of the patriarchs (Abraham, Isaac, and David), shepherding was considered a noble profession.

At the time of the prophets, shepherds symbolized judgment and desolation. In this Old Testament prophecy, the shepherd functioned as judge to separate the sheep from the goats:

As for you, my flock, this is what the Sovereign LORD says:

I will judge between one sheep and another, and between rams and goats. (Ezekiel 34:17).

Jesus later said something very similar in his "Parable of the Sheep and Goats" Matt. 25:31–46). In both cases, the sheep represent God's people and the goats represent those who have rejected God. At the end-times judgment Jesus will be the ultimate judge:

> *Then he will say to those on his left, 'Depart from me, you who are cursed, into the eternal fire prepared for the devil and his angels'. (Matt. 25:41)*

Bad Shepherds in Ezekiel

Ezekiel 34 had a lot to say about bad shepherds of Israel who did not take appropriate care of their flocks. God became very angry with those bad shepherds and said that not only would he be against them but also, he would actually replace them:

> *The word of the LORD came to me: ² "Son of man, prophesy against the shepherds of Israel; prophesy and say to them:*
>
> *'This is what the Sovereign LORD says: Woe to you shepherds of Israel who only take care of yourselves!*
>
> *Should not shepherds take care of the flock? ³ You eat the curds, clothe yourselves with the wool and slaughter the choice animals, but you do not take care of the flock.*
>
> *⁴ You have not strengthened the weak or healed the sick or bound up the injured.*
>
> *You have not brought back the strays or searched for the lost.*
>
> *You have ruled them harshly and brutally. ⁵*
>
> *So they were scattered because there was no shepherd, and when they were scattered they became food for all the wild animals. ⁶ My sheep wandered over all the mountains and on every high hill. They were scattered over the whole earth, and no one searched or looked for them.*
>
> *⁷ "'Therefore, you shepherds, hear the word of the LORD: ⁸ As surely as I live, declares the Sovereign LORD, because my flock lacks a shepherd and so has been plundered and has become food for all the*

wild animals, and because my shepherds did not search for my flock but cared for themselves rather than for my flock, ⁹ therefore, you shepherds, hear the word of the LORD

¹⁰ This is what the Sovereign LORD says: I am against the shepherds and will hold them accountable for my flock. I will remove them from tending the flock so that the shepherds can no longer feed themselves. I will rescue my flock from their mouths, and it will no longer be food for them.

By the first century, shepherds stood at the bottom rung of the social ladder. The Mishnah belittled shepherds and one passage stated that there was no obligation to rescue a shepherd who'd fallen in a pit. Among the religious leaders, shepherds were often given the label "sinners" which was their technical term for a class of despised people.

The Bad Shepherd Became the Good Shepherd in Luke 15

Recall the opening line of the first story, *"Suppose one of you has a hundred sheep **and loses one of them** ... "*. Jesus was asking the Pharisees to put themselves in the place of the bad shepherd in the story. Jesus didn't waste any time; the very first line portrays the shepherd as a "bad shepherd" because *he lost his sheep.* The language of the parable clearly placed the responsibility/blame for losing the sheep squarely on the shoulders of the shepherd, not the sheep itself. Even though Jesus was only talking about losing one sheep, there was no "wiggle room" for the shepherd. He was responsible ... period.

Since the Pharisees would never consider themselves to be "lost" (and they refused to humble themselves enough to identify with the shepherd), they could only identify with the ninety-nine sheep. But the ninety-nine were not really players in the story. Thus, by default, the Pharisees were forced to identify with the least important characters in the story. This was another insult to their pride.

There weren't a lot of rules about shepherding, but this one was crucial: *"Don't lose any sheep"*. Sheep were valuable to the village, and any "good" shepherd would do whatever it took to find a lost sheep and bring him back. The shepherd couldn't return home without all of his sheep (or at least a partial carcass if an animal had gotten the sheep); that would have been a very shameful and cowardly thing to do, and might well have gotten him beaten, stoned, or banished from the village if he tried such a thing. No, recovering the sheep, no matter how difficult that task may be was his duty, his responsibility, and everyone knew that.

Because the Pharisees were excellent students of Scripture, they would have recalled a similar story about other "bad" shepherds in the Old Testament. They would have remembered the Ezekiel 34 passage wherein God expressed his anger toward *the bad shepherds of Israel.*

The Pharisees would have understood that Jesus was comparing them to the shepherd, and they would have been highly offended, especially being compared to the bad shepherd! They thought themselves so much better than these unclean sinners! As far as the Pharisees were concerned, shepherds were the dregs of the earth. There's no way a Pharisee would ever become a shepherd – *not even in their imagination*! And to be compared to not just any shepherd, but the **bad** shepherd, the Pharisees would have immediately taken great offense at Jesus' call to adopt such a humiliating position. Further, they would have remembered how angry God was at the bad shepherds of Israel in the Ezekiel 34 passage, and they knew that they were considered shepherds of Israel. The weight of Jesus' condemnation must have been heavy indeed!

Shepherd's Wilderness

The key characteristic of the desert, from the perspective of our parable, is that one is separated from God – or, in this case, the God-figure of the shepherd – and, therefore, the "sheep" is very vulnerable and in a dangerous place.

As soon as the bad shepherd recognized that a sheep was missing – and – he decided to go search for the sheep, he began his wilderness experience, the completion of which would find him transformed into the good shepherd.

As the "bad" shepherd changed his perspective from self-interest to caring for the sheep, and as he took the necessary actions to find and restore the lost sheep, he became the good shepherd. The good shepherd would have had to go out into the Judean Desert to search for his lost sheep; putting himself at risk as he did so.

Shepherds would have pastured their sheep close to the village in the springtime, but as the year wore on, the nearby pasture would have become exhausted and the shepherds would have had to take their sheep farther out into the desert to feed. Over the summer, the desert produced a form of hay, which the sheep could eat. It wasn't the preferred pasture, but it would fill the sheep's stomachs and keep them alive. This was, most likely, the setting where the shepherd found himself with his lost sheep.

The shepherd's wilderness experience occurred in a literal wilderness – probably the Judean Desert, which was a very rugged and barren land. It had hills and canyons ranging from 1000 meters in the mountains to 420 feet below sea level at the Dead Sea (the lowest point on earth). It had very little vegetation because it received only about two inches of rain per year. There would have been miles and miles of pure desolation; deep ravines and rocky terrain. Since it was so desolate, there were very few people, but it did attract the outcasts, fugitives, robbers, thieves, and even, on occasion, fearful rulers such as David. Consequently, the shepherd would have had to worry not only about the cliffs and rugged terrain and animal predators, but also human ones who might try to steal the sheep.

Jesus' audience would immediately have understood the wilderness the shepherd had to search, as they would have remembered the stories of the Israelites wandering in the desert for 40 years. They would have recognized a wilderness as a place set apart that forced the people to confront their own hunger, fears, and isolation while forging a spiritual connection with God. (Ex. 15-20)

The Good Shepherd

The good shepherd would do what was necessary. He would certainly go searching for any sheep that got lost, and if necessary (probably), he would carry the sheep back home on his shoulders. (A sheep could easily weigh up to one hundred pounds.)

This story also places the responsibility for finding the sheep solely on the shepherd. The Pharisees knew that too. Even though they had no use for those lowly shepherds, they understood the ethical obligations of a shepherd. They could have understand the recovery of the lost sheep from an economic and ethical standpoint, but to connect that recovery to joy in heaven over one sinner who repented would probably have gone completely over their heads.

As he transformed into the good shepherd, he became a symbol for the Good Shepherd, Jesus Christ. In the Old Testament, it was Yahweh who was called the Good Shepherd, but in the New Testament, Jesus claimed to be the Good Shepherd (John 10:14): *"I am the good shepherd; I know my sheep and my sheep know me."* That was the statement that caused the Jews to think he was demon-possessed. Later, in verse 25, he told them they were not his sheep; it was that statement that caused many in his audience to pick up stones to stone him, for they considered these statements to be blasphemy.

Jesus was a good shepherd, but he wasn't just an ordinary good shepherd. When he said, *"I am the good shepherd"* (John 10:11), he was making the fourth of his seven "I AM" declarations. The "I AM's" specifically pointed to his unique, divine authority and purpose.

The Pharisees would have recognized that God alone was referred to in the Old Testament as the "Good Shepherd." They would have immediately thought of Psalms 23 *"The LORD is my shepherd …"*.

Although the Pharisees would have understood that the Old Testament referred to God as a good shepherd, they couldn't understand why God (or Jesus, in this parable) would choose to compare himself to such a lowly outcast member of society, a sinner, an unclean person. This idea of God taking the initiative to seek and save the lost would have been a new idea to the Pharisees. They held a very low opinion of shepherds in general, and weren't even sure that they should be saved, or even rescued from a pit.

The Pharisees would have recognized that by making these associations, Jesus was identifying himself as God. The considered that claim to be blasphemy, and they were so outraged by his claims that they increased their opposition to him.

The Bad Woman Became the Good Woman (God Symbol)

The Bad Woman

The second story opens much like the first: *"Or suppose a woman has ten silver coins and loses one."* Again, Jesus wastes no time getting to the point – here was a woman trusted to handle her family's money and she lost one of her valuable coins.

The woman is responsible for losing the coin - it would be ridiculous to consider that a coin could lose itself! Again you see that it's the caretaker who has lost something, and it is the caretaker who is responsible for the loss.

The second story– with a woman as the main character – would have been shocking, if not scandalous to Jesus' audience. They would have understood the low status of women under their patriarchal system, and all the men would have been offended by Jesus' use of a woman as a main character in this story. It was considered highly offensive for anyone to use a woman as an analogy when speaking to a male audience such as the Pharisees, teachers of the law and the tax collectors, and the Pharisees would have been highly offended to be compared to a woman. Jews often prayed, *"Thank God that I was not born a woman."*

Although Jesus was inviting his hearers to put themselves in the place of the main character of each story, the Pharisees simply would not have been able to do so. As hard as it would have been for them to imagine themselves as a lowly and unclean shepherd, they would never have been able to imagine themselves as a woman in this story.

The Woman's Wilderness

The woman's wilderness experience started when she realized she had lost the coin, and it ended when she found the coin. Her "wilderness" consisted of the dark, dusty space inside her home, with a floor made either of basalt stones stretched across the floor or a dirt floor covered with plants. Either way, it would have been quite dark and required diligence and perseverance to find the lost coin.

Darkness symbolizes the wicked, death, judgment, misery and adversity, everything anti-God. Dust is similar in that it symbolizes humiliation, punishment, mourning, extreme affliction, and the grave. Clearly, being in the dust and the dark is not a desirable place to be.

The Woman's Wilderness Experience

You have the lost coin in a dark house, lying in the dust, and waiting for the woman's sweeping (cleansing action) to find and recover it. The lost object is totally unable to find itself, to repent, or to return home on its own. The coin, like the sheep, is totally dependent upon the seeker to persist in the search until found.

The woman's wilderness experience would have started as soon as she realized the coin was missing, and it would have continued until she found the coin and restored it to its proper place.

The first thing the woman did was to reach for the light; the light is important to the story. In the Bible "light" is always good, and it always symbolizes the removal of darkness. It's also used as a symbol for life, salvation, the commandments, and the divine presence of God (Ps. 56:13; Is. 9:2; Prov. 6:23; Ex. 10:23).

Then she began to sweep the floor looking for the coin (Luke 15:8b). The sweeping represents a cleansing process. Like the good shepherd, the good woman is a responsible person – she has been entrusted with her family's money and she accepts the responsibility for finding the coin that was lost. Like the good woman described in Proverbs 31, she has integrity. She admitted responsibility for losing the coin (she could have kept it a secret, and no one would have known) and she was diligent in her search to recover the lost coin.

Unlike the shepherd, she knew where the coin was – it was somewhere in the house, and so, with sufficient effort, she would find it. Recovery of the coin was totally up to her – there was no way that the coin could "find itself." The woman would need to be both diligent and perseverant in order to find the coin, but at least she knew that it was lost inside the house.

The Good Woman (God Symbol)

As the woman did all the necessary things like gathering the light and sweeping the floor, she would eventually find the coin, and as she did, she became the good woman, another God symbol in this parable.

The story of the woman and the lost coin represents the Son's mission (remember, the focus of the story is the woman, not the coin). The woman was the seeker, and she carried with her the light. Jesus said,

"I am the light of the world ..." (John 8:12). Light symbolizes a holy God, his presence and his favor (Ps. 27:1; Is. 9:2). The New Testament uses that symbol for Jesus 72 times.

The "Bad" Younger Son Became the "Good" Son (Jesus)

The third story started a bit differently: *"There was a man who had two sons ...".* This is a much longer story and there are more characters involved. There's the father, the younger son and the elder son as main characters. All of these main characters are human, and as such they are active agents, making ethical and moral decisions and choices, based upon their own psychological and spiritual needs. There are three locations: the father's house, the distant country, and the father's fields. The timeframe is much longer than it was for either of the two previous stories – the younger son was probably gone for two or three years, based on the famine account.

Younger Son Is a Complex Character

The younger son is a very complex character. The ambiguities inherent in his story require the audience to fill in the gaps. Perhaps that's why there are so many varied interpretations. This story has a lot to say about psychological and theological issues such as: identity, intimacy, election and covenantal relationships. A lot of spiritual questions are addressed throughout the story, by multiple characters; some are answered, some are not. Jesus embedded a number of "open loops" in this story, leaving it up to his audience to supply the answers.

The rabbis in general, and Jesus in particular, told parables that had implied referents to the Old Testament, and they expected their audience would be able to make the necessary connections. That's what Jesus has done with this parable – only the implied referent is not so much the Old Testament, but rather, the implied referent was Jesus' person and his kingdom of God ministry (happening in real time, before their eyes).

Younger Son Was Elected

It appears that the younger son was elected, as evidenced by the final outcome of the story. Looking at this story from a theological (election) perspective, it seems that the father bypassed the firstborn, who was culturally most worthy of election (primogeniture), and chose the younger instead (James 2:5; I Cor. 1:27f).

Election is totally a reflection of God's sovereign will and his choice to select one individual, but not another. "Works" will not ensure election (as the elder son discovered), but one who is elected will inevitably demonstrate good works, as well as obedience and trust in God.

Because the younger son was elected, the father knew he would return home eventually, he just didn't know when. Consequently, father carefully monitored the road leading into the village, and constantly watched for his son's return. He didn't interfere with his son's departure, or his son's experience while away from home, because he was a freedom-giver. He patiently waited for his son to return of his own volition, without forcing or coercing him.

From the standpoint of election, we know that God's sovereignty will ensure that all those who have been elected will persevere to the end. Jesus assures us that he won't lose anyone:

And this is the will of him who sent me, that I shall lose none of all those he has given me, but raise them up at the last day. (John 6:39)

When the son returned because of his ultimate trust in his father, the son's actions demonstrated his election. His father's exuberant welcome reception provided further evidence. Jesus' earthly ministry and the younger son's journey show many parallels, far too many to be coincidence; they had to be part of Jesus' intended message. Those parallels strongly reinforce the conclusion that the younger son represented Jesus. Over the course of the story, the younger son transformed from a bad son who had broken relationship with his father to a good son, representing Jesus, who had restored relationship with his father.

Covenant is the basis for human relationships. The new covenant and the kingdom of God are related concepts. Just as love is central to human relationships, God's love is central to the New Covenant. Human beings were made to be part of a community; we were not meant to live in isolation, we need each other. Families, church and community all provide opportunities for developing and maintaining relationships.

Family Life Cycle – Launch Phase

This story describes two sons who have encountered a family situation distressful enough that one felt the need to leave home and travel to a distant land and the other felt the need to spend his time out in the fields with the hired hands. At the beginning of the story, the family clearly had not resolved these issues and had not achieved any sort of balance between separating and belonging.

From a family life cycle perspective, this event represents the launching phase wherein a young adult leaves home to in order to define a "self" in relation to the family of origin. It includes finding a job and accepting emotional and financial responsibility. In our parable, the family was launching the younger son; however, that launch wasn't totally successful as he ended up returning home. But it wasn't a total failure either, as he grew and matured during his time away from home.

Younger Son's Request

The third story starts off with the younger son making an unusual, counter-cultural request of his father – and, amazingly, his father granted that request! From the patriarchal perspective, this request is outlandish, unheard-of, almost criminal, but from the kingdom of God perspective, it looks entirely different.

Several words in this story are crucial to its interpretation – "prodigal", 'substance", "squander", "wild living" and "came to himself". We need to determine what they mean before drawing any conclusions about this passage.

No Motivation Given for the Request

At the beginning of the third story, the younger son made the following request of his father: *'Father, give me my share of the estate.''* Based on nothing more than this short statement, many analysts impute all sorts of nefarious motives to the boy (he's greedy, he's selfish, he wanted his father dead) – *but the text says absolutely nothing about his motivation.*

Is he a bad son? Maybe, or maybe not, but we can't know from this one short sentence. The only thing we do know is that he asked for his inheritance.

The younger son "acted out" (in the sense that he took action) and left home; he physically left his father's house and went far away. He moved from being "present but not available", to "not present and not available", and finally, to being "both present and available" for relationship. His choice, which took a detour through the distant country, was still a good choice because it resulted in eventual restoration to the family and his ultimate five-fold blessing, with rewards and elevation in status as his father's son and heir.

While many authors try to impute negative motives to the younger son, the text gives no information at all regarding the younger son's motivation. It is just as likely that, given the frequency of famines in the area, that the younger son decided to emigrate to another location that had better opportunities, as had many of his peers. We simply have no way of knowing what his motive was, since the text doesn't tell us.

Jesus Taught Disciples to Ask

What we do know is that Jesus had previously taught his disciples to ask freely of God (Luke 11:2-3). It appears that the son was merely following Jesus' teaching, and while making this request of his father was a novel concept for the Pharisees, it was legal and not a sin. This was just another one of Jesus' challenges to the existing legalistic, patriarchal culture.

When he finally became so hungry that he wanted to eat the pods he was feeding the pigs (very bitter and difficult, if not impossible, for the human body to digest!), he decided it was time to go back to his father's house where he would at least get fed. But, that was a risky decision because he knew he would likely have to face the *kezazah* "shame" ceremony before he could reach his father's house. That would cause him to be cut-off and probably chased out of the village, with – or without – rocks and sticks doing the talking. But, he had enough faith in his father that he knew it would work out, somehow.

Younger Son Was Not a Prodigal

Even though this story is frequently referred to as "The Parable of the Prodigal Son," this third story should not be considered a standalone parable, and the word "prodigal" does not even appear in the text. Some translator or interpreter has made an inference along the way. The word "prodigal" means one who has been "driven out." From all appearances, the son left voluntarily – at a time of his own choosing; he was not "driven out." It is an erroneous inference, but unfortunately, one that has been propagated by many subsequent reviewers.

Substance or Property (ousia)

One of the words that is important to understand in this story is "substance". The word [*ousia*] typically translated "property" could just as easily, and more correctly be translated "substance". The word is derived from the verb "to be" [*eimi*]. The other word used for that which was distributed [*bion*] means life, means of living, sustenance, maintenance, substance, or goods. When the son left, he took all that he had; he took *his "substance"*, his *"being (from eimi),"* his *"life (bion)"* (Luke 15:13).

His "substance" was effectively the provisioning for his journey to the distant country, which is what any prudent person would do.

When I wrote this section, my city was experiencing a major flood from Hurricane Harvey. The people in my neighborhood were under mandatory evacuation orders so many of us packed up our families, our pets, and necessary supplies to carry us through the duration of the evacuation. It only made sense to take as many supplies as we could because we didn't know when we would be able to replenish our stores, or if we might need to share supplies with others who were less fortunate.

We left our homes behind because survival was at stake. This evacuation was only a temporary measure, but it was a necessary one. Some of the people who evacuated ahead of the flood came home to find their houses and possessions were still safe and dry. Others, however, came back and found their houses with a foot or more of water. Furniture was damaged. Cars were swimming in the floodwaters. A few people even found that the structure of their home had been damaged from the wind. Sometimes, your life's path takes some unexpected twists and turns. But if you stay true to your calling, you will eventually find your way back home.

Younger Son's Wilderness

His wilderness was the far country. His wilderness experience began when he left his father's house and it ended with the healing meeting with his father at the village outskirts.

The essence of the "distant country" is that it is totally separated from the father's presence. The Greek phrase used can be interpreted as a euphemism for dying. As soon as the son left home, his father considered him both "lost" and "dead". (Notice: he's lost and dead from the father's perspective, not from the son's perspective.) The distant country represents a place where evil exists and flourishes. The distant country is a place we have all visited; it's where we were born (Rom. 3:23).

The distant country is a testing ground, a rite of passage that must be endured, and mastered, on one's own. The important thing about the distant country is that it always presents you with a choice; it's life at the crossroads. You have temptations to face and choices to make.

The younger son grew and developed as he progressed through his journey. This story demonstrates the actuality of the younger brother's sonship (he was elected) **before** he had actually claimed his position in the family.

Did the Boy Sin?

Many interpreters jump to the conclusion that the younger son sinned while on his journey, but what was his sin? The only things the text reveals about his activities are 1) he requested his inheritance, 2) he spent all his money, and 3) he hired himself out to a Gentile farmer and fed pigs. None of those things is a sin; counter-cultural, yes, but not a sin.

Asking Is Not a Sin

Some argue that merely making his request of the father was a sin, but they base that conclusion on patriarchal cultural norms, not on Jesus' intended message. The son merely made a simple request of his father, one that his father could easily have rejected. He didn't steal his inheritance nor did he deceive his father. He made a simple, straightforward request.

The patriarchal father was all-powerful within the family; he would not have had any problem saying "No" if that was what he wanted to do. Nor would the typical patriarchal father have allowed his son (especially a younger son) to force him into any action he didn't want to take.

Asking is not a sin, especially not when you look to Jesus' ministry for the answer instead of patriarchy. Jesus actually commands his followers to ask (Matt. 7:7-12). Earlier, Jesus had taught his followers to *"ask, seek, and knock"* and then promised to satisfy their needs (and he even used a father-son analogy!):

> *So I say to you: Ask and it will be given to you; seek and you will find; knock and the door will be opened to you.* ¹⁰ *For everyone who asks receives; the one who seeks finds; and to the one who knocks, the door will be opened.*

> ¹¹ *"Which of you fathers, if your son asks for a fish, will give him a snake instead?* ¹² *Or if he asks for an egg, will give him a scorpion?* ¹³ *If you then, though you are evil, know how to give good gifts to your children, how much more will your Father in heaven give the Holy Spirit to those who ask him! (Luke 11:2-13)*

Feeding Pigs Was Not a Sin

While the younger son was in the distant country, he ran out of money, so he found a job slopping pigs for a Gentile pig farmer. Once again, Jesus introduced a very counter-cultural situation, which would certainly have been very humiliating for a Jewish boy, but not a sin. Eating pork or touching a pig carcass was prohibited, but merely feeding the animals wasn't:

> *The pig is also unclean; although it has a divided hoof, it does not chew the cud. You are not to eat their meat or touch their carcasses. (Deut. 14:8)*

Younger Son Was Not Recklessly Spendthrift

After inferring the negative word "prodigal" commentators pile on further negative meaning by assuming that prodigal meant "wayward." But according to Merriam-Webster's Collegiate Dictionary, it means *"recklessly spendthrift"*. In addition, Webster's New World College Dictionary gives this meaning: *"extremely generous; lavish; prodigal with one's praise"*.

What if you were to assume that the boy was "extremely generous; lavish" with his money while on his trip, rather than "recklessly spendthrift'? Would that change your understanding of the parable?

Squandered Means Scattered

The word describing his action is translated "squandered." This is probably not the best translation for those words. First the word "squandered:" the Greek word is *diaskorpizo, which means scattered*.

I grew up as a farm kid and when I hear the word scattered, I think of the many times I helped plant garden and certain seeds you just scattered while other seeds you actually planted. I also think of the many times I've seen someone sitting on a park bench scattering some bread crumbs for the birds to eat. Is this necessarily a wasteful or reckless action on the part of the one who is "scattering"?

God Wants People to Give Generously

Ecclesiastes Chapter 11 reminds us of the benefits of "scattering":

1 Cast your bread upon the waters, for after many days you will find it again.

2 Give portions to seven, yes to eight, for you do not know what disaster may come upon the land. ...

6 Sow your seed in the morning, and at evening let not your hands be idle, for you do not know which will succeed, whether this or that, or whether both will do equally well.

Matthew henry's Commentary explains Ecclesiastes 11:1-6 this way:

Solomon presses the rich to do good to others. Give freely, though it may seem thrown away and lost. Give to many. Excuse not thyself with the good thou hast done, from the good thou hast further to do. It is not lost, but well laid out.

God is lavishly generous and wants his people to be generous also:

Now to him who is able to do immeasurably more than all you ask or imagine, according to his power that is at work within you, ... (Eph. 3:20).

God consistently wants people to give generously, so generously in fact, that many might consider it "thrown away and lost" or "wasteful" or "reckless." In these examples, it seems that the scattering is being done with the expectation of a positive return and that God is generous beyond your wildest dreams.

Younger Son Was Not Immoral

Many reviewers go on to assume that just because he traveled to the distant country (some Gentile area that raised pigs), he automatically sinned while he was there, but there is no evidence in the text to support that conclusion.

Next, consider the word translated here as wild is the Greek word *asotos*. It does not really mean "wild"; rather, **it means expensive ... and with no hint of immorality**! Bailey states,

*With the one exception of the Old Syriac, your Syriac and Arabic versions for 1800 years have consistently [sp.] translated "expensive" or "luxurious" or "spendthrift living," **with no hint of immorality.***

The word translated "wild living [*asotia*] is derived from the negation of the word [*sozo*] meaning to save. His "wild living" could be viewed in the same way as Jesus' willingly giving up his own life (i.e., "not saving" his life) so that he could save ours.

Elder Son's False Witness

The elder son did accuse the younger son of squandering the father's money with prostitutes, but this is merely an unsupported claim by a less than objective witness. Was the elder son a companion on the journey? Did he actually witness the younger son's behavior? (It does not appear so.) He would not have had any way of knowing what his brother did – or did not do – while he was away.

On the other hand, did the elder son harbor feelings of anger and jealousy toward his brother? Did he have any hidden agenda or ulterior motive that would have given him reason to impugn the character of the younger son? (Very likely, yes). So ... how trustworthy a "witness" is the elder son in this matter? Should you accept the elder son's comments without any corroboration?

It does not appear that the elder son personally observed any of the younger son's behavior, and there were no other witnesses yet the traditionalists seem very willing to accept the elder son's comment (which was likely to have been either/both meddlesome or slanderous) as sufficient proof to condemn the younger son.

Younger Son Did Spend His Money

There have been many accusations made against the younger son, but in reality, the only valid one is that he spent all his money. Note: he spent *his* money; money that he had every right to spend in any manner he saw fit.

Therefore, the son scattered his wealth to the Gentiles through expensive living with no hint of immorality! That gives an entirely different feeling than saying he threw his money away through wild and reckless behavior, doesn't it?

The Younger Son "Came to Himself"?

During the course of his journey, the younger son fell upon hard times. His money had run out, and the area was experiencing a severe famine. He found himself hungry, in a desperate situation, and no one would help him. It was at that point that the younger son *"came to himself."*

What does it mean to say that the boy *"came to his senses"* or some versions say *"came to himself"?* Obviously the younger son found neither satisfaction nor fulfillment from his work feeding the pigs (i.e., industry), because that was not his calling, nor his mission in life. His mission was to serve his father in faithfulness and obedience. Once he realized that, he returned home to his father, to seek his grace and compassion.

He knew he had been living as a false self, because he had not yet grasped his true identity – he was still trying to relate to his father through his works (just like his brother); as a servant or a hired hand, but not yet as a son and heir

It's All a Matter of Perspective

The boy was not a "prodigal". He didn't wish his father dead (at least we have no textual evidence that he did). He didn't steal from – or deceive – his father. He wasn't immoral. He wasn't recklessly spendthrift. The words "squandered" and "wild" don't mean what you might first think they mean. Rather, *they reflect God's generosity to mankind.*

What really is the difference between giving generously and throwing money away? Whether one is being generous and philanthropic, or someone is wasting and squandering his money is largely dependent upon the evaluator's subjective point of view. Whether something is expensive but justified, or wasteful is really a value judgment.

Consider that perhaps, the younger son like Jesus, didn't spend his money in a wasteful manner – but in an extravagantly generous manner because he was a man commissioned by his father for a greater purpose.

So whose judgment about the inherent worth or value of a thing should you accept? Jesus' and God's assessment, or man's assessment – especially when the man making the assessment may have an ulterior motive, like the elder son?

God gives generously to those who are in relationship with him. David pictured God as a rich and generous man who gives indiscriminately to all people (Ps. 36:7).

Did He Repent?

Some interpreters take that he "came to himself" to mean he repented. But did he? Typically if the Bible were to speak of repentance, it would have used the word "*shub*" instead of "*nefesh*," which would have indicated that he returned to God. But in this story the younger son "*came to … himself*"… not to his father, and not to God. Bailey draws a distinct contrast between how the younger son came to himself (i.e., his *nefesh* came to his own *nefesh*) as opposed to how David returned to God; i.e., his *nefesh* returned to God, not himself (Ps. 23). Bailey goes on to say that none of the twelve hundred year history of Arabic versions translates this phrase as indicating repentance.

Younger Son Didn't Repent

The younger son says, "*Father, I have sinned against heaven and against you …*" (Luke 15:18). Although this statement sounds very sincere, it really wasn't; there's no emotionality to go along with that statement, no awareness of any actual sin against his father or against God. And, the statement itself is a quote from a line that Pharaoh used on Moses trying to persuade him to end the plagues (Ex. 10:16).

The Pharisees would have recognized that reference to Pharaoh and the intended manipulation. The younger son's single goal was to find food for his belly, and he knew that there was food at his father's house.

Parallels Between Jesus and the Younger Son

There are a large number of parallels between Jesus' earthly ministry and the younger son's story – far too many for them to be mere coincidence. In this section, we'll explore those parallels.

- Both fathers approved the son's journey.
- Both sons took their "substance" as provisions for the journey.
- Both sons left a comfortable home to go on a difficult trip.
- Both sons suffered a great deal while they were on their mission.
- Both sons reached a point where they realized their true identity and calling.
- Both sons returned to their father.
- Both sons were welcomed, celebrated and elevated to higher positions than when they had first left home.

Both Fathers Approved Their Sons' Journeys

Jesus' Father explicitly approved his earthly ministry (Heb. 10:7, John 6:38). In fact, he commended Jesus publicly and with an audible voice at his baptism: *"You are my Son, whom I love; with you I am well pleased."* (Mark 1:11)

Whereas God the Father had been explicit in his approval, the younger son's father implicitly approved his son's trip when he distributed his inheritance – distribution required positive action on the father's part. He didn't need to ponder the request or debate the pros and cons – he granted the request immediately (barely a heartbeat between the request and the distribution). We can legitimately conclude there was implicit approval since the father had to take positive action to grant the son's request. (Luke 15:12)

Both Sons Asked Their Fathers for Their Substance

Jesus didn't come in the role of slave to a master, but he came in the role of son to a "daddy". They had such an intimate relationship that

Jesus could ask his father for anything. Jesus did not asking for something outrageous, but something his father had already commissioned him to do. By recognizing Jesus as the prodigal son and God as the Father, we can see that God gave of his very being – he gave of himself – to a world that was lost and sinful. Nouwen states,

Jesus is the prodigal son of the prodigal Father who gave away everything the Father had entrusted to him so that I could become like him and return with him to his Father's house.

Both Sons Took Necessary Provisions for the Trip

When Jesus left heaven, he took what he needed for the journey on earth – he took on the form of mankind (John 14:1). Jesus' receipt of the Holy Spirit was a necessary step of "provisioning" for his public ministry. Jesus knew from the very beginning of his journey (before it even began), that completion of the mission would cost his very life (i.e., all of his substance). John the Baptist called Jesus the Lamb of God:

The next day John saw Jesus coming toward him and said, "Look, the Lamb of God, who takes away the sin of the world!" (John 1:29)

And Jesus said, *"I am the good shepherd. The good shepherd lays down his life for the sheep"* (John 10:11).

What more extravagant gift could there be than for one who had no sin to "become sin" for you so that you might enjoy eternal life with God in heaven?

The younger son needed his inheritance (or "substance," or "life") to accomplish his mission as well. The word used for that which was distributed [*bion*] means life, a living, sustenance, maintenance, substance, or goods. This was a necessary provisioning for the mission, and the father recognized that, which is why he granted the request.

Both Sons Had a Wilderness Experience

Immediately after his baptism, the Holy Spirit led Jesus into the wilderness to be tempted by Satan (Luke 4:1-13). Jesus defeated Satan on all points, and did not succumb to sin. It was also the time that really solidified Jesus' identity as the Messiah.

The younger son's wilderness experience occurred primarily in a Gentile land like Jesus'. His journey didn't result in literal death like Jesus'; however, his father did consider him dead and then alive upon his return home.

Both Sons Suffered

Immediately after his baptism, the Holy Spirit led Jesus into the wilderness (some versions say "drove him") – and why? So that he could be tempted by the devil for forty days. The devil threw everything he could at Jesus, but he passed every temptation by using the Word of God, for which Satan had no answer.

Jesus experienced life as a human being, and he experienced all the pain, suffering, and feelings that are part of the human experience. His suffering was physical, emotional and spiritual. Jesus suffered mightily on his journey to the cross, but that doesn't mean that he had taken the wrong path; rather, it served to confirm that he was actually on the right path.

The younger son seemed to be suffering family conflict at home, so he left only to encounter more suffering on his journey. He suffered criticism, rejection, humiliation, hunger, and even character assassination upon his return.

Both Sons Spent All Their Substance

Jesus spent his entire substance when he died on the cross and rose again to save mankind.

"Christ Jesus, who, being in the form of God, ... humbled himself and became obedient to the point of death, even the death of the cross" (Philippians 2:5-8).

The younger son spent **his** money; money that he had every right to spend in any manner he saw fit.

Both Sons Had Extravagant Tastes

Jesus accepted extravagant gifts. For example, he allowed two women to anoint him with expensive perfume, and both times someone challenged that action as being wasteful. Yet Jesus defended the action and even forgave one of the women's sins as a result.

Further, he taught his disciples not to worry – and advised them to *sell their possessions and give to the poor*, trading treasures on earth for treasures in heaven (Mark 10:21).

The younger son lived expensively, but not recklessly.

Both Sons Were Rejected and Criticized

Jesus was rejected and criticized throughout his ministry – but, just because he was criticized doesn't mean that he sinned.

- His family thought he was out of his mind (Mark 3:20-21).
- He was rejected because he was "just" a carpenter's son (Mark 6:3).
- Whole towns pleaded with him to leave their region (Matthew 8:34).
- The people in the synagogue drove him out of town and wanted to throw him off a cliff (Luke 4:28-29).
- The Pharisees criticized him for healing on the Sabbath and consequently they plotted to kill him (Mark 3:1-6).
- The Pharisees and scribes criticized him for not ceremonial washing before eating (Mark 7:1-8; Matthew 15:1-2).

- He was accused of being a "glutton and a drunkard."
- The teachers of the law criticized him for forgiving sins (Mark 2:1-7).
- The teachers of the law criticized him for eating with sinners and tax collectors (Mark 2:16).
- He was rejected in favor of Barabbas (Luke 23:18).

The younger son was criticized for everything from making his initial request, to turning the inheritance into cash, living in a Gentile country, losing his money, working for a pig farmer, and returning home empty-handed and penniless.

Both Sons Were Rewarded for Passing Their Tests

Jesus clearly passed his tests, starting with Satan's temptations in the wilderness and ending with his death and resurrection. His ascension back to heaven and the right hand of God provided his reward.

The Bible tells us that there can be rewards for those who successfully *"pass the test"* (James 1:12, I Peter 1:7). The younger son's father gave him the best robe, a signet ring and sandals. By these actions, the father was re-affirming his approval and love (with the robe), his riches (with the ring), and his sonship (with the sandals).

Conclusion: Jesus As the Prodigal Son

The younger son's journey paralleled Jesus' earthly ministry in many key respects. By recognizing Jesus as the prodigal son and God as the Father, we can see that God gave of his very being – he gave of himself – to a world that was lost and sinful. According to Nouwen,

Jesus, the Beloved of the Father, left his Father's home to take on the sins of God's lost children and bring them home. But, while leaving, *he stays close to the Father and through total obedience offers healing to his resentful brothers and sisters. Thus, for my sake, **Jesus becomes the youngest son** ..."*

After Jesus completed his mission, God rewarded him for a job well done. Nouwen paints you a picture of Jesus as the prodigal son:

he [Jesus] cried out 'Yes, I am ascending to my Father, and your Father, to my God, and your God.' And he ascended to heaven. Then in the silence, looking at his Son and all his children, since his Son had become all in all, the Father said to his servants, 'Quick! Bring out the best robe and put it on him; put a ring on his finger and sandals on his fee; let you eat and celebrate! Because my children who, as you know, were dead have returned to life; they were lost and have been found again! My prodigal Son has brought them all back.' They all began to have a feast dressed in their long robes, washed white in the blood of the Lamb.

Kingdom of God Explains Father's Compassion

If you use Jesus' teachings instead of patriarchy, especially those regarding the kingdom of God where the values of grace, forgiveness, humility, servanthood, sacrifice and love predominate, it is much easier to understand a father wanting to spare his son the shame of undergoing the *kezazah* ceremony. His actions prevent the ceremony from occurring and restore the son's dignity and respect in the eyes of the community. The father traded his shame and humiliation for his son's, just as Jesus has done for all of us.

The younger son could be with his father because he had been forgiven. John says that we can enjoy the same fellowship with God as Jesus did. (I John 1:1-3)

Younger Son's Return

Integrity answers the question, "How will I be whole (or saved)?"

God is the source of your personhood. To be and become a "self" requires development within each of the four tasks of identity, intimacy, industry, and integrity. Integrity involves becoming a whole through the discovery, acceptance, and nurturance of your selves as spiritual beings because people stand in relationship to a transcendent and personal God.

Since God created us in his image as relational beings, the only way we can experience our true humanity is through a relationship with the one who created us. Our identity as believers derives from having been "elected" by God. Realization of self requires realization and acceptance of your role as a son or daughter of God, and co-heir with Jesus. Amazingly, the Bible describes the actuality of your existence before you were even born:

> *For you created my inmost being ... all the days ordained for me were written in your book before one of them came to be (Ps. 139:13-15)*

The pursuit of integrity always occurs in interpersonal contexts, with God understood as a personal being. According to John 17:3, you were made to know God and be an heir and joint-heir with Christ.

By the end of the story, the younger son had reached out and reconnected with his father (God). The returnee's desire for restoration and reconciliation was stronger than his fear, or he would never have risked the trip. He needed a good sense of self, and a lot of trust in his father (i.e., a covenantal relationship) to return home.

We can see from the younger son's actions that he had a secure attachment to his father and a covenantal relationship. Knowing that helps to explain both why the son would take the risk to return home after losing all his money to Gentiles and also, why the father would run to meet his son – at the edge of the village (before the elders could perform their *kezazah* ceremony).

The customs of the day would have called for severe punishment for his behavior. The younger son would have known about the *kezazah* ceremony (in fact, he would have known that was a risk before he ever decided to leave home); consequently, he should have expected to be greeted by a group of angry villagers.

This was a "ceremony of shame*" designed for the younger son's exact situation*. This ceremony was performed when a Jewish man left the community, went and lived with the Gentiles, and lost his wealth. When he came back, he would go to the city gates and the older men would throw down a pot in front of the young man - symbolizing the broken relationship that now existed between the community and this 'sinner.' Sometimes this ceremony would have escalated into beatings, or worse. This ceremony separated him from his family, his community, and his faith and demonstrates the importance they put upon relationships, loyalty to family, and not getting involved with Gentiles. He would be permanently cut-off, ex-communicated from the community.

If the *kezazah* ceremony had occurred, irreparable damage would have been done. By meeting him at the edge of the village, the father was able to protect his son from the *kezazah* shame ceremony.

It appears the younger son had a strong relationship with his father, secure attachment, or a covenantal relationship. Psychologists have found that youngsters having secure attachment to their parents are more adventurous and willing to explore their environments. They tend to be more independent, more resilient, more self-confident, more sociable, and more moral than children with insecure attachments. Even though the younger son opted to leave, when it came time to return, he had sufficient courage and confidence in his father that everything would work out. As time passed, the younger son felt the call of belonging (and also, the desire for a full belly), so he decided to return home.

Eschaton (Final Goal in Creation)

The story of the man with two sons demonstrates the paradigm of human personhood, in all its ramifications: the need for affirmation, for belonging, for restoration and healing, for being a significant person and for not being forgotten.

The younger son went on his "heroic journey" – a difficult journey of self-discovery, but it seems in the end, he found himself. The younger son "came to himself" meaning he had discovered and accepted his identity, thus he was able to go home to his father and accept his true identity as son and heir. We see change, growth, development and maturity as a result of his journey. His father recognized that newfound maturity in him, and elevated him to a position of full adulthood. He gave him the robe of honor, the ring of power, and the sandals of wealth.

Realizing self is another instance of a "promise" becoming reality. The younger son had matured on his journey and was now ready to accept his adult responsibilities as a son and heir to his father's fortunes. This was evidenced by his father's response to him – a five-fold blessing (five being the number of grace).

Intimacy and industry converge in the need to love and to work. God tells you, *"For I know the plans I have for you, plans to prosper you and not to harm you ..."* (Jer. 29:11). The younger son had a higher calling in life than feeding pigs, and once he realized that, he returned home to fulfill his role and mission in life.

The father was a freedom-giver; he empowered his sons to grow and mature – to develop their own personalities, gifts, abilities and yes, opinions and beliefs. He even allowed them to make their own mistakes. He respected them enough to allow them to choose freely whether to love and obey him, or to go their own way.

The father offered the younger son his love, compassion, forgiveness, and acceptance – and by the feast, he re-established their relationship.

This enabled the younger son to assume his rightful position as son and heir.

Intimacy answers the question, *"To whom am I close?"* or *"Who is close to me?"* Identity must be solidified before it can be shared with another in an intimate relationship. (In other words, you can't share something you don't have.) Genuine intimacy requires mutual self-disclosure; you can only know another insofar as they allow you to know them. The younger son felt the need for relationships, for intimacy, love, forgiveness, and grace. The younger son accepted the invitation to relationship.

Identity is inextricably related to intimacy, for one discovers one's identity in the context of relationships, and the family is God's specifically designed laboratory for learning about relationships. Episodes of belonging and separating form the foundation of being and becoming a self. Others act as mirrors in which you can see yourself better and more objectively.

God discloses himself through divine revelation, which is essentially intimacy, i.e., the sharing of self with another. To be open to finding wholeness through experiencing God in your lives is to be open to experiencing intimacy. You realize this intimacy through forgiveness and acceptance.

Rather than starting with the patriarchal father and trying to imagine what your heavenly Father is like, Jesus has given us the ultimate definition of godly fatherhood. All we have to do is look at the relationship between Jesus and his Father – that's the model for us as well. Packer writes,

God intends the lives of believers to be a reflection and reproduction of Jesus' own fellowship with Himself.

In the Bible, meals represent fellowship, acceptance, and reconciliation. (That's why the Pharisees were so upset about Jesus eating with the tax collectors). God's invitation to a meal, especially the Last Supper, is an invitation to intimacy. There he says to his disciples,

> *I tell you, I will not drink from this fruit of the vine from now on until that day when I drink it new with you in my Father's kingdom. (Matt. 26:29)*

The younger son could co-exist with a holy God because he had been forgiven. When you acknowledge God and enter into relationship with him, that relationship contributes to your being able to discover and solidify your identity, as you experience separateness and belongingness in the relationship.

When the father met his younger son at the village outskirts, he was creating the time and space whereby healing could occur through the reality of their person-to-person meeting. He was creating a real relationship – one full of risks as well as rewards, sorrows as well as joys but a relationship that was both real and intimate.

Reconciliation is the restoration of true humanity through the new humanity of Christ. Paul tells us that we have received the adoption of son and that we are no longer slaves, but heirs.

The younger son received blessings far and above what he was expecting. He depended upon grace, not law, and he allowed God to be God. He realized that he was not in the place of blessing, and he was not where God wanted him to be to complete his mission and accomplish his purpose in life.

Home Is Where You Accept Your Identity

Home is where you accept your identity, and the younger son was able to fully engage and enjoy the benefits of being "home." According to Nouwen,

> *The younger son's return takes place in the very moment that he reclaims his sonship, even though he has lost all the dignity that belongs to it*

Theologically and psychologically, you need to come to grips with your dark side – whether you call that side "the old man" or "the shadow," you must resolve the tension between the good and the bad we all carry within ourselves. Jung contended that a conscious integration of your shadow is essential if you are to establish human relationships. Further he saw the person-to-person relationship as the vehicle through which the patient discovers:

> *that his own unique personality has value, that he has been accepted for what he is, and that he has it in himself to adapt to the demands of life.*

Initially, the younger son acted out, but he grew and matured throughout his wilderness journey. He was able to recover his true self. The younger son did not identify himself with the difficulties of his life, his "mistakes," his developmental milestones; he identified himself as a son and was wiling to assume his calling as heir. He was ready to assume the responsibilities of adulthood and maturity. He was ready to move on to the future.

He was able to come to terms with his identity; and therefore, claim his "self". This identity relates to his prior election. In claiming his true self, he was able to establish his integrity as well. When he returned to his father, he was able to realize his long hoped-for intimacy with his father. As a son and an heir, he had a mission into which he could fully invest himself.

Bad Father Transformed into The Good Father

The father is an interesting character, and one who acts counter-culturally, just as the younger son had done, and also just as Jesus had done throughout his public ministry. He demonstrated many feminine characteristics, such as compassion, and acted in ways that a woman in first century might have acted, but a man would never do.

The Bad Father

The father agreed to the boy's request and distributed his estate – to both his sons. Unfortunately, that meant the younger son would leave home, and consequently the father had effectively "lost" that son.

The Pharisees and many others in Jesus' audience would have been scandalized that the father acceded to the son's "outrageous" request. They would have thought that he had violated his duty to the family by giving the early distribution of the estate.

Further, they would have considered his behavior to be totally inappropriate for a proud, patriarchal father – the son should have run to him, not the other way around. And they would have been scandalized at the gifts the father gave the returnee, given tradition would have said he should be punished severely.

Many of them may have felt empathy for the elder son – after all, he was the firstborn and should have been entitled to double the inheritance and the best blessing.

The Father's Wilderness

The Father's "wilderness experience" started when his younger son left home, and ended when the son showed up at the village outskirts. From the time of his departure, the father considered his younger son not only lost, but also "dead". His suffering was primarily mental and emotional, worrying about his son and hoping that he would return home soon. In the meantime, he had another troubled son still living at home who had simmering anger issues, chose to withdraw from his father, and isolated himself out in the fields rather than spend time with his father. Eventually, the elder son's anger issues burst to the surface, exacerbating the relationship issues between the two of them and his brother. Effectively, the father lost the older son as well as the younger one.

Good Father

The good father represents God and Jesus. Few would argue with viewing the father as God; this seems to be the one point of commonality between the many interpreters of this passage. According to Packer, God's fatherhood of Jesus implies four things: authority, affection, fellowship, and honor.

In this story, Jesus redefined what it meant to be a good father. God as parent, stands above masculine and feminine roles, encompasses both, and sets the pattern for Christian parenting.

God and Jesus demonstrate the ultimate in receptivity; the feminine character of God includes her openness, sensitivity, the ability to let go, to be fully present, hospitality, healing through meeting, discernment, patience, caring, vulnerability, compassion, gentleness, and the ability to rest in God. Because God is love, s/he experiences deep grief and suffering when his/her children stray far from home: s/he actively seeks them out and when they return, or are found, s/he rejoices!

God as father is a freedom-giver: he allowed both sons to make their own choices concerning their life paths and to suffer the consequences of their choices. He did not prohibit their choices, nor did he override them – or their consequences.

Father Pleaded With Elder to Enter In

He also pleaded with his eldest to join the family in celebration, but the boy refused (Luke 15:28-30). If he had entered the father's banquet hall, he would have needed to treat his brother the way his father treated both of them.

Being in the Father's house requires that I make the Father's life my own and become transformed in his image.

It's curious why the father didn't press his invitation – it was customary for the host to keep asking until the guest finally agreed. And, it's also curious that the son couldn't find some way of accepting his father's invitation (which was probably more like an "order" than a true invitation).

Elder Son Did Not Transform

The elder son was totally missing during the first half of the story, without any explanation. As the elder son, the audience would have expected to hear from him before they heard from his younger brother (who spoke from the very beginning).

Notwithstanding the audience's expectations, he should have spoken up and tried to mediate the conflict between his father and his brother before it got out of hand (that was one of the responsibilities of the eldest son).

Or if he felt as strongly about his brother's request as it appears at the end of the story, he should have raised his objections when the request was first made.

The elder son had never ventured off like his brother did. He stayed with his father and he "did his duty," much like a hired hand or a slave or a servant. We're not told exactly what he was doing all this time, but it seems safe to believe that he had been working in the fields, just as he was doing when his brother returned.

The elder son working in the field is reminiscent of both Cain and Esau who were men of the field (Gen. 4:2; 25:27). In the Old Testament, Israel was supposed to be a priest to the nations, to represent and pray for the Gentiles in the Temple. By working in the fields like Cain and Esau, Jesus is saying that the elder brother had lost his mission, much like the Pharisees who had rejected God's call upon their lives.

The phrase "draw near" (Luke 15:25) is a technical term used in Leviticus for when Israel "drew near" to the Temple for worship. The elder son, like Israel, came in from the field and saw that the "sinners" had come into the Temple (his father's house). Although his father (God) was happy that his younger son (Jesus) had come back, and he provided him with a whole new wardrobe, indicating a priestly role, the elder son was jealous, angry and bitter. He seemed to think it should be his decision rather than his father's as to who was welcome in the father's house and who was not.

Elder Son Was Not Elected

This parable demonstrates that not all who hear God's message respond and become part of God's family. Both the elder son and the younger son grew up in the same home, they heard the same messages, but they made different decisions about life, their mission and their calling as sons and heirs.

The elder son appears not to have been elected. From his actions and attitudes, it seems that the elder son hadn't been adopted out of "slavery" because he hadn't accepted his father's values. His attitude and disobedience would prevent his admittance to the kingdom just as they had prevented his entrance to the party. His pride did not allow him to enter into the celebration, for to do so, he would have had to reconcile with his brother, and he simply was not willing to do that.

Even though he was the firstborn, his father skipped him and directed his attentions, his gifts and his blessings to the younger son. From his complaints, it appears that he never had his father's signet ring that would have authorized him to buy and sell in his father's name (i.e., he had never claimed his sonship), and we know he never had a fatted calf to party with his friends (or even a small goat).

Elder Son Denied His Sin

Gal. 5:19-21 lists a series of sins that prevent people from inheriting the kingdom of God, and the elder son seems guilty of many of them:

The acts of the flesh are obvious: sexual immorality, impurity and debauchery;[20] idolatry and witchcraft; hatred, discord, jealousy, fits of rage, selfish ambition, dissensions, factions [21] and envy; drunkenness, orgies, and the like. I warn you, as I did before, that those who live like this will not inherit the kingdom of God.

The elder son's "non-existent" sins were many:

- He committed the unforgiveable sin of unbelief.

- He failed to perform his duty as mediator between father and son at the very beginning of the story, and it's likely that he failed to perform his duty as priest to the Gentiles throughout the story. He kept saying that he'd "done his duty" – but had he really? He seemed to be pretty much out of touch with reality.

- Like Adam (Gen 3:8-10), he seemed to want to hide from his father by spending his time out in the field, and therefore, away from his father's presence. It appeared that he was afraid to be around his father, and afraid to speak up at the beginning of the story.

- He was very angry with both his father and his brother. *"But I tell you that anyone who is angry with his brother will be subject to judgment"* (Matt. 5:22)

- He accused his brother of sinning with prostitutes when he had no way of knowing what his brother had, or had not done, while he was away. Thus, he was either providing false witness, or projecting his own guilt onto his brother (or both).

- He shamed his father further by completing refusing his invitation, which would have been considered a rejection of the person offering the invitation.

- He disobeyed his father's orders; he should have helped with hospitality and hosting duties.

- He shamed his father by refusing to come into the party and then, by shouting at him in a public setting.

- His pride and self-righteousness would not allow him to enter into the celebration or connect with either his father or his brother.
- He refused to admit his sin, to seek forgiveness or reconciliation.
- He rejected relationships with both his father (God) and his brother (Jesus).

"He who does not honour the son does not honour the father who sent him." (John 5:23)

- He further dissociated himself from the family by saying, *"this son of **yours**"*.
- He refused to be adopted out of slavery into sonship. He didn't appear to trust his father's goodness, or even to be interested in having a real relationship with either one of them. Therefore, according to Jewish law and custom, he ***sinned***.
- He rejected his rightful identity as son and heir, and he preferred to operate in the role of a servant or hired hand. He apparently hoped to win his father's approval through his work, rather than his being.
- By staying out in the field, he avoided his rightful mission.

Why didn't the elder son find some way to accept his father's invitation? And, by refusing to join the party, the elder son declared his rejection of both his father and his brother. Elder son's response to the family conflict situation was to withdraw and isolate from the family. The elder brother gave up on relationship; his pride was more important than his family. Ego was more important than intimacy, and ambition was more important than obedience.

It's important to keep the divisive nature of Jesus' parables in mind. Whenever a dichotomy is presented (two's of anything), Jesus is pushing his audience to make a decision; choose one side or the other. As Heb. 3:1–18 says,

And to whom did God swear that they would never enter his rest if not to those who disobeyed? So you see that they were not able to enter because of their unbelief. It still remains that some will enter that rest, and those who formerly had the gospel preached to them did not go in, because of their disobedience.

The partygoers would have been surprised that he didn't receive severe punishment for disrespecting his father.

Even the Pharisees realized that even if they had been able to live up to the law, including their oral traditions, they still would have no relationship claim upon God:

So you also, when you have done all that is commanded you, say 'You are unworthy servants; you have only done what was your duty.' (Lk. 17:10)

Elder Son's Wilderness Was the Field

The wilderness isn't always a physical place; sometimes it's an emotional one. It frequently symbolizes mental and physical barrenness. The *teknon* doesn't seem to be at all creative or be able to figure out a way to have a party with his friends – even though he's just received his share of the estate.

He seemed to be using the field as an escape; somewhere he can be separate from his father. When he was in the field working as a slave or a servant rather than in the house, he didn't have to deal with either his father or his brother.

Although his father had called him "son" [*hios*] at the beginning of the story, by the end of the story, he simply referred to him as "child" [*teknon*], a relatively impersonal term, emphasizing his lack of maturity, understanding, responsibility and authority. He appears to be still operating as a child:

What I am saying is that as long as an heir is underage, he is no different from a slave, although he owns the whole estate. ² The heir is subject to guardians and trustees until the time set by his father. ³ So also, when you were underage, you were in slavery under the elemental spiritual forces of the world. (Gal. 4:1)

He was not ready to assume his adult responsibilities. He wasn't mature, and he couldn't forgive. He couldn't accept the developmental changes in others as they grew and matured, and he wouldn't allow himself to mature. He just wanted to stay where he was – as a "slave" and a "child". He didn't seem to understand that acting like a servant who merely obeyed orders wouldn't earn his father's love or approval.

Elder Son Rejected Identity as Son and Heir

The elder son rejected his identity as son and heir, but he hadn't chosen another identity. Since he had never left home, in any real sense, and he had never really separated from his father emotionally or developmentally, it wasn't possible for him to make a free choice to return.

The elder son had not found satisfaction in his work either – even though he was already dutifully and obediently serving his father. Since he had not yet discovered his identity, no mission could be matched to his nebulous identity. From his actions and attitudes, it is clear that the elder son had not accepted his position as son nor his role as co-heir. He hadn't been adopted out of "slavery" because he hadn't accepted his father's values.

God said the plans he has for us are *"plans to give you hope and a future"* (Jer. 29:11b). Further, in Zech. 4:6, he says, *"without a vision the people perish."* The elder son was lacking all three of those things: hope, a future and a vision.

The elder brother viewed himself as a martyr or a victim. He was still playing the victim card, even though he had received his share do the estate at the same time as his brother. He could only focus on the so-called "injustices" of his life; the past rather than the future. Because he was so caught up in the past, he could not even enjoy the present.

Elder Son Liked the Darkness Better than the Light

The elder son seemed to have been afraid to go into the light of the father's celebration. Why did the older boy get so angry and feel the need to withdraw? He received his fair share of the family fortune. His place in the family was not threatened by anything his brother had done. (Perhaps the light may have exposed his hypocrisy and self-righteousness.)

Light has come into the world, but men loved darkness instead of light because their deeds were evil. Everyone who does evil hates the light, and will not come into the light for fear that his deeds will be exposed (John 3:19).

Elder Son Did Not Transform

One of the purposes of this parable was to divide its hearers into two groups: those who understand and believe versus those who don't understand and/or don't believe.

The elder son is unique among the primary characters. He had not grown or matured during the course of the story, if anything, he'd regressed. He was angry, rejecting, disrespectful and playing the victim card, even though he, like his younger brother, had already received his share do the estate. His pride and his anger kept him from joining the festivities or reconciling with either his father or his brother (who represented Jesus). Thus, the elder son rejected both God the Father and Jesus the Messiah.

At the end of the story, the elder son just stands sulking in the dark … where does he go and what does he do? The parable doesn't tell us. But, it certainly seems to fit the description of the "distant" country (maybe not physically, but definitely emotionally and spiritually) as a place where he would be out of fellowship with God (i.e., his father and his brother).

Many commentators associate the elder son with the Pharisees and certainly he does represent them. In a sense, though, the elder son also represents Adam who typifies fallen humanity (Rom. 7:7ff). He didn't appear to trust his father's goodness, which was the same basic sin that caught Adam (Gen 3). When Adam heard God in the garden (after he and Eve had sinned), he hid from God because he was afraid (Gen 3:8-10). Likewise, the elder son seemed to need to get away from his father. (Whereas Adam hid from God in the garden, the elder son hid from his father by spending his time in the fields.)

He also represents all those who do not believe in Jesus or obey God and who, consequently miss out on the blessings of the kingdom of God.

CONCLUSION

The Transformation Parable

We looked at the parable Jesus told, as recorded in Luke 15. This was one of Jesus' more complex parables: He used a very unique storytelling technique wherein the characters changed and developed during the parable. He included five key characters, five different "wildernesses (or deserts), three different timeframes, and three different homes. Just looking at the number of variable involved makes it easier to understand why there have been so many varied interpretations of this passage.

Three Stories, One Parable

The parable, which I'm calling *"The Transformation Parable,"* included these three stories: the shepherd who lost his sheep, the woman who lost a valuable coin, and the man with two sons. Many people look at each of these stories as a standalone parable, but doing so doesn't agree with how Jesus categorized them in his answer to the Pharisees. He clearly stated that the three stories comprised one single parable.

Unique Storytelling Device: The Characters Transform

Each of the main characters started out with a "bad" persona; they had either lost something, or they, themselves, were "lost." However, during the course of their respective stories, each of the main characters changed, grew, developed, and "morphed" into a "good" persona. The single exception to the transformation rule was the elder son whose character remained relatively static, in fact, he probably regressed during the story rather than exhibiting any growth or maturity. The good personas came to represent both God and Jesus, in their roles as seekers who find and save the lost; thus significantly enlarging the Jewish view of God. Thus, God became the composite of the Good Shepherd, the Good Woman, the Good Father, and the Good Younger Son.

The elder son did not become a God figure, rather he came to represent first of all, the Pharisees in the audience who had suffered a failure of leadership, but he also became a symbol of all people who reject God and Christ.

Five Key Characters

The five characters include the shepherd, the woman, the father, the younger son and the elder son. The Pharisees considered shepherds to be much like the tax collectors: lowly, unclean and the dregs of the earth. They considered women to be at the bottom of the social scale, and many Jews were known to pray to God thanking him that they had not been born a woman. In first century Israel, a woman ranked very low on the social ladder and had very little power or authority. The Pharisees would have had enough trouble trying to put themselves in the place of those unclean shepherds, but when Jesus asked them to picture themselves as the woman who had lost her coin, they simply would have refused. There was no way they were going to liken themselves to a woman, even in their imaginations!

Then we come to the story of the man with two sons. Even though interpretations of this passage vary widely, pretty much everyone agrees that the father in the story represents God. However, as we come to find out, he also represents Jesus! (That is a bit difficult for many to grasp!).

Five Wildernesses (or Deserts)

The Bible tends to use the symbols of the wilderness and the desert interchangeably (depending upon the translation). Regardless of whether we talk about the desert or the wilderness, they both represent an isolated, liminal space where God can get our attention, exercise divine discipline; develop a secure attachment and a real, intimate, covenantal relationship. God uses the desert to refine his children, removing the "chaff" of life so that they become what he predestined them to be.

The Shepherd's Wilderness / Desert

For the shepherd, his wilderness was a literal one, most likely the Judean Desert – a very harsh, hostile environment with miles and miles of desolation, hills and valleys, many cliffs with sharp drop-offs, very little water, and almost no vegetation. (Rainfall was only about two inches per year.)

In general, sheep represent God's people; in this case, the lost sheep represented a sinner in need of saving. The shepherd was the seeker who found and saved the lost sheep.

His wilderness experience would have started as soon as he realized that his sheep was missing and it would have continued until he found the sheep and got it safely back to the sheep fold in the village. During the course of his wilderness experience, he might have faced many dangers: heat, thirst, falls, wild animals, or even robbers and thieves who might have wanted to steal his poor lost sheep. Once he found the sheep, it would have been so traumatized that the shepherd would probably have needed to carry the sheep home; it wouldn't have been able to walk on its own (and those sheep would often weigh about one hundred pounds). So, his journey would have been both difficult and dangerous.

The Woman's Wilderness

For the woman, her "wilderness" was the dark, dusty interior of her home, with black basalt floors (or dirt floors covered with reeds, etc.) and very little light. The only "windows" in her house would have been small circular windows or three-inch slits high up off the ground. They were designed more for ventilation than for light and an exterior view. Consequently, no matter the time of day, it would have been dark in her house.

The woman's "wilderness experience" would have started as soon as she realized the coin was lost, and it would have continued until she had found the coin and restored it to its proper place. She had an advantage over the shepherd in that she knew where the coin was — it was somewhere inside her house. But the dust and the dirt and the darkness made it difficult for her to find the coin. Her search would have required diligence and persistence, but eventually she would have found the coin.

The darkness, dust, light and the broom are both significant symbols in the woman's story. In order to find the coin in the dark, the first thing she did was to reach for the lamp, and the next thing she grabbed was a broom to begin sweeping the floor in search of the coin.

Darkness represents everything that is opposed to God, the wicked (Prov. 2:13), judgment (Ex. 10:21), and death (Ps. 88:12).

The dust represents shame, humiliation (Ps. 72:9; Micah 1:10), and spiritual death and the grave (Job 7:21). To sit in the dust, as did the lost coin, represented extreme affliction. When someone was in the dust, they were as low as a person could go.

The light has been used throughout the Bible in contrast to the darkness, and it always defeats the darkness. It represents the holy God, God's presence and favor, and the revelation of his love (Ex. 10:23; Ps. 27:1;Is. 9:2; II Cor. 4:6; I John 1:5-7), goodness, truth, life (Ps. 56:13), and salvation (Is. 9:2). Jesus is referred to as the light of the world (John 8:12; 9:5).

The broom symbolizes cleansing. The woman diligently searched and cleansed her house looking for the lost coin.

The Younger Son's Wilderness

The younger son's wilderness was the time he spent in the far off Gentile land. His wilderness experience began when he claimed his inheritance prematurely, and it ended when he returned to his father's house and re-claimed his sonship.

The son's wilderness was filled with all the things the Jews considered sinful and detestable: Gentiles, whom they hated, pigs which they considered unclean, all kinds of sensual temptations and ways to fritter away one's fortune.

In the son's case, he also encountered a severe famine and no one would give him anything to eat. Thus, just like the shepherd's wilderness, food was scarce. Things got so bad for the boy that he even considered eating those bitter pods that were fed to the pigs. His hunger finally drove him to return home to his father.

The Father's Wilderness

The father's wilderness was primarily an emotional and spiritual desert, not a literal one. He did not suffer from hunger or heat or harsh physical environments, but he did suffer from the loss of his son and heir. His was an experience of grief, shame for the way their relationship had deteriorated and broken in front of the whole community. He missed his younger son and his heart broke, awaiting his return. (The father had elected him, so he knew he would return sometime, he just didn't know when.)

The father's heart was also broken due to the estranged relationship he had with his other son. The elder boy seemed not to want to spend any time in his father's presence, and he even seemed to be intimidated by him; consequently, he spent most of his time out in the field with the hired hands. Thus, both boys were effectively lost to the father, and he grieved for them both.

The Elder Son's Wilderness

The elder son appeared to be "lost" from the very beginning of the story. He should have been present and involved with his brother's request to divide the estate, and considering how angry he was at the end about that, he should have raised his objections before the distribution occurred.

But, apparently, he spent most of his time out in the field with the farm hands. This is reminiscent of both Cain (Gen. 4:2) and Esau (Gen. 25:27) who were both farm hands. He seemed to need to avoid his father's presence (or hide from him, as Adam had hid from God after he had sinned). Adam's basic sin, (Gen. 3), like that of the elder son, was unbelief – not believing in the goodness of his father (God).

He was angry, jealous, self-righteous and in denial. He was spiritual dead in his wilderness. Further, in the Old Testament, Israel had an obligation to be the priest to the nations (Gentiles), to represent and to pray for them in the Temple. By hiding out in the field, the elder son has abdicated his priestly mission.

He claimed that he had never sinned and that he always "did his duty," yet he failed to act as mediator between his father and brother at the beginning of the story, he failed to enter into the party at his father's invitation (order) at the end of the story, and he rejected both his father and his brother. He preferred to stand outside in the dark, rather than enter into the light of the party. (Perhaps he had a guilty conscience he didn't want discovered?)

He referred to himself as a servant or slave, and seemed to think that his "work" would earn his father's affection and approval. He represented the Pharisees in the immediate audience, who also thought they could earn God's favor through their works. The elder son, like the Pharisees, was self-righteous and believed he had never sinned, yet his actions and his attitudes demonstrated otherwise. But the son also represented all the people who reject God and Jesus, starting with Adam.

The elder son was clearly a "half-full" kind of guy. He spent a lot of time complaining, worrying about the things he didn't have, rather than being grateful for the things he did have, and being jealous of his younger brother.

The older son, the firstborn, should have been the one receiving the biggest share of the estate – and the biggest blessing from the father – but that didn't seem to be the case. We know he had never received a fatted calf from his father – or even a small goat – and, it appeared that he had never been entrusted with the signet ring of familial authority. He clearly had not accepted his role as son and heir, he refused relationship with both his father and his brother, and consequently, he was never adopted into the kingdom; he was not elected.

Three Timeframes

There were also three different timeframes: the woman could have found her coin in an hour or a day, at most. The shepherd would have found his sheep in at most a couple of days (if it took him longer than that, the sheep would have died). The boy's journey, however, took much longer. Given the reference to a severe famine in the land, exegetes believe he was gone for at least a couple of crop cycles, or two to three years.

Three Homes

The Sheep Fold

Once the shepherd had his flock safely back home, they would stay in a sheepfold, or sheep pen for protection from any dangers of the night.

Historically, a sheepfold would have a rock wall, possibly with thorns across the top. It would have an open area for the sheep to come in and go out. The shepherd would lie across the opening at night to prevent thieves, robbers and predatory animals from getting to the sheep. Jesus said that he was the gate for the sheep:

Very truly I tell you Pharisees, anyone who does not enter the sheep pen by the gate, but climbs in by some other way, is a thief and a robber. (John 10:1)

The Woman's House

The woman cleansed her house using the light and the broom for her floor, much like Jesus cleansed the Temple of the moneychangers. The woman's house represented the nation of Israel and the lost coin those who were elected. This was God's house, one he had built and dwelt in for a long time. But those of the elect were out of sight, lost in obscurity and darkness, with dirt and reeds on top of them. They were in need of saving, yet they could not save themselves. They were, however, capable of being recovered – and that depended upon the efficacy of the woman's sweeping and cleansing activities.

The Father's House

Old Covenant Temple

In the Old Testament, the father's house (God's house) would have been the Temple, which was a physical replica of God's heavenly dwelling (Ex. 25:8). The Levites were the ones chosen to serve God, and the priests were selected from the tribe of Levi.

Jesus is our high priest and both the father and the younger son represent Jesus, therefore, both must have been priests serving in the Father's house, the Temple. The father sacrificed the fatted calf as a sin offering for his younger son. Since he had been feeding pigs, which were considered unclean animals, he would have been considered ceremoniously dead.

The calf was a sacrificial animal in the Old Testament used as a sin offering (Lev. 9:2-8), and the new clothes the father gave his son suggest some form of ordination for priestly services in his father's house, the Temple. The Bible defines a priest as follows:

A chosen officer or prince with the capacity to draw near to God and minister. He alone is responsible for offering the divinely appointed sacrifices to God, for executing the different procedures and ceremonies relating to the worship of God, and for being a representative between God and man.

New Covenant, Kingdom of God

Home in the kingdom of God is the place where we accept our identity (Matt, 11:28; John 14:23). It is the place to which every Christian aspires. It is the place of eternal security and rest. According to Nouwen,

Home is the center of my being where I can hear the voice that says: 'You are my Beloved, on you my favor rests.

Jesus Confronted the Pharisees with their Failed Leadership

The Pharisees, who hated Jesus, were always looking for ways to trip him up and discredit him, and this situation was just one more opportunity for them to try to do that. They criticized him for eating with tax collectors. They thought that indicated Jesus had a low view of sin and sinners, which they couldn't condone.

The Pharisees (and most of the Jews) thought the tax collectors were unclean, unworthy, criminals and completely dishonorable people. They were hated and despised because they collected those onerous taxes on behalf of the Romans. Not only did they collect the taxes that were due but they added extra amounts on top of the actual bill, and kept the excess for themselves. Even the rabbis wouldn't have anything to do with them. They weren't allowed in the Temple, and no one would even take their money because it was considered tainted. The Pharisees, known as Separatists, wouldn't have anything to do with them for fear of defiling themselves.

Jesus responded to their criticism by telling them three stories where the main character in each story represented himself; therefore, he responded by describing himself as a shepherd, a woman, a father, and a son who had left home and traveled to pagan country before returning to his father and receiving rewards from his father.

The Pharisees struggled to comprehend what Jesus was trying to tell them. They knew about shepherds; everyone did. Shepherds were very common in first century Israel. They understood that Jesus was portraying them as the bad shepherds in this parable, and their training in the Scriptures led them to realize that he was also making a reference to the bad shepherds in Ezekiel 34. The bad shepherds in Ez. 34 were the "shepherds of Israel," and the Pharisees really got it. They clearly understood that Jesus was painting them as the "bad shepherds," and they also understood from the Ezekiel passage exactly how angry God was with those bad shepherds.

But, the Pharisees put shepherds in pretty much the same category as tax collectors – "low lives" that they avoided at all costs. They were offended to be portrayed as shepherds, and doubly offended to be considered as the "bad" shepherds.

Jesus didn't mince words or cater to the feelings of the Pharisees. He had been criticizing them for their pride and hypocrisy throughout his ministry, and this parable simply "doubled-down" on that criticism. After portraying them as bad shepherds, he asked them to picture themselves as the woman who had lost a valuable coin. As far as the Pharisees were concerned, matters had just gone from bad to worse – now Jesus was asking them to picture themselves as ... of all things ... *a woman!* As difficult as it would have been for them to picture themselves as a lowly shepherd, for the Pharisees to picture themselves as a woman was impossible! (Their anger and offense meter would have skyrocketed by now!)

Transformation

The purpose of doing the interpretation was simply to uncover the themes of transformation and sanctification in the parable. Each of the main characters transformed from a negative persona (having lost something, or being the lost one) to a positive persona (the seeker or finder of the lost object). This represented a big change, so how did it happen?

The Wilderness Experience Is Key to Our Spiritual Growth and Maturity

This parable provide a number of lessons we can learn, and principles we can derive, regarding wilderness experiences that will help us in our daily lives. First and foremost, we need to recognize that these wilderness experiences are God's preferred tool for sanctifying his children. God's style is to lead his chosen people, his children, into the isolation and barrenness of the desert or the wilderness (physical or emotional). He's used them throughout history with kings and prophets and heroes of the faith; we should not be surprised when he invites us into the wilderness for our own private tutorial.

Wilderness Characteristics

Wilderness Experience Is Customized Just For You!

God deals with each of us in a very personal and unique way; the wilderness experience is perfect for that task. God provides all believers with their own "wilderness experience" at some point in their lives (sometimes more than once!). The desert concentrates our focus on the things that matter while removing much of the "noise" of modern life. It provides a place of solitude, a time for reflection, and a space where God can get our full attention.

Sometimes, It's a Refuge, a Safe Haven

Sometimes God leads us into the wilderness to protect us from an abusive or otherwise evil situation. It can be a place of escape, refuge and seclusion. It becomes a safe haven for us, just like it was for David when his enemies were chasing him.

Other Times, It's a Harsh Testing Ground

The wilderness can be a harsh and dangerous environment, but trust in God and he will get you through. No matter how difficult the tests or challenges he presents, he promises to never leave you or abandon you. He may remain hidden, silent and invisible from you for a time to give you the opportunity to exercise free will, but he has not abandoned you.

God likes to pick a location that is isolated from the hubbub of our daily lives; one where there is quiet and solitude so that you can hear his still, small voice. The wilderness is a place of encountering God; he speaks to us in the wilderness.

It Brings Disruptive Changes

No matter how God chooses to use the wilderness in our lives, it will undoubtedly cause major changes in our everyday lives. Perhaps we will have to relocate, possibly even change our names, take a totally different kind of job, or simply spend some time in a hospital or rehabilitation center, just recovering. Regardless of its exact nature, it will be a disruptive change, one that will require a period of time to assimilate the changes and transition to our new life in a new environment. The person leaving the desert will not be the same one who entered it; the experience will have changed us.

The Old Rules No Longer Work

The wilderness is a "Neutral Zone" where the old rules and procedures no longer work, but new ones haven't yet been put into place. The wilderness always presents choices; it's life at the crossroads and it creates opportunities and new beginnings. You just need to have the courage to leave the past behind and pursue the new life God has prepared for you.

Wilderness Goals

God Wants to Establish an Intimate Relationship With Us

God wants to have a real, intimate relationship with us. Human beings see God as an attachment figure; we find our purpose, meaning and security in him. Attachment Theory tells us that stress is a necessary ingredient in the attachment process, resulting in secure attachment with God.

I'm sure most of us would like to avoid all such wilderness experiences, but they seem to be God's preferred way of dealing with him people, so expect your invitation will be coming soon (if it hasn't already arrived). No believer can avoid the wilderness experience.

God Wants Us to Trade Self-Reliance for Dependence on Him

Many wilderness experiences are about God teaching us not to rely upon ourselves, but to trust and depend upon him. To ensure that we learn that lesson, he will frequently remove the things that we currently use as "crutches" to maintain our self-reliance: jobs, spouses, family, friends, houses, cars, savings and retirement accounts. He wants us to love him for who he is, not for the blessings and "toys" that he gives us. In some cases, people have become so reliant upon these things that they've become "idols." God is a jealous God and he doesn't want you to have any idols at all.

God Wants You to Become Spiritually Mature

God will use this intimate, one-on-one time in the desert to refine you, to remove the "chaff" and emotional baggage that you might be carrying, and anything else that prevents you from becoming the person he created you to be. This refining process may at times be painful and involve suffering, but just like a surgery in the physical realm, removing toxic elements from our lives results in an overall benefit.

Transformation Happens in the Wilderness

God loves wildernesses and deserts, and he's used them throughout history to mold and shape many of the heroes of the faith, including: Moses, Elijah, Jeremiah, David, Job, John the Baptist, Peter, Paul and even, Jesus. Each of them had life-transforming experiences in the desert.

Moses and the Israelites experienced God's divine discipline because of their disobedience. It took them 40 years in the desert to eradicate the sin from the midst, thus enabling them to enter the Promised Land.

David visited his desert experience on three different occasions, and each time, there was an important lesson for him to learn. As a youngster, he was growing and learning while he tended his flock. He learned to use the slingshot that later brought down the giant, Goliath. He also mastered the harp and other musical abilities while in the desert, and he was able to use his skills to calm the evil spirit that possessed King Saul (I Sam. 16:14-23). His second tour of the desert was when he fled King Saul (1 Sam. 19:18-27:6), and the third time, King David entered the Judean Desert as a refuge while fleeing his son Absalom's revolt against him. It was during this time that he wrote Psalm 63.

When Elijah had his turn in the wilderness, he learned that God was not in the fire, or the earthquake or the wind, but his was a still small voice that required focus and quietude to hear. It was there that he got his marching orders, among them to anoint Elisha as his successor.

John the Baptist spent 30 years in the desert under God's tutelage for his very important six-month ministry introducing Jesus to the world, in his public ministry. God raised him up to call people out of Pharisaic Judaism with all its rules and legalism, but none of the heart and spirit of the kingdom. God used the desert to strip away all the unnecessary and unhelpful trappings of a religion that had gone off-track. He was developing some "clean slates" that Jesus could mentor and use to communicate his message to the masses.

The Holy Spirit led Jesus into the desert right after his "mountain-top" experience of baptism and hearing his father audibly commend him and approve his mission. Here Jesus defeated the enemy, Satan, and solidified his identity. He was being branded as the right interpreter of the Law, in the mold of Moses; therefore, those who followed Moses must now follow Jesus. It was necessary for Jesus to be severely tested before beginning his public ministry. He defeated Satan's tactics and succeeded where Israel had failed. He also drew closer to his father during this time. When he left the desert, he left in power, and recognized that he was fulfilling prophecy (Luke 4).

Wilderness Principles

God Has Orchestrated Our Wilderness Experience

No matter how difficult our journey, we need to remember that God has orchestrated our desert experience – for our benefit – and he has a plan for that time. God may use family, social or political conflicts to send you into the wilderness. We also need to remember that he doesn't think of time the same way we do; he thinks and plans for eternity, while we tend to think and plan for today – or possibly – tomorrow. Remember how long Moses and the Israelites were in the desert. I imagine those years seemed quite long to many of the people; however, every minute of that time was necessary for God's plan to be realized.

God Loves Us Unconditionally and He Has a Plan

God loves us unconditionally and he wants what's best for us. If you're in the wilderness today, be glad; it's because God is transforming you. The best thing we can do in the desert is to cooperate with God. Don't fight him and don't try to run away or escape from the experience. Trust God to accomplish his perfect will in your life and trust him also to take care of you while you are in the desert.

You Have to Leave Your Old Life Behind

Entering the wilderness means leaving your old life behind. God is doing something new in our lives, and one of the reasons he takes us out to the desert is so that we leave all our old "baggage" behind. The wilderness is a place where God uses positive divine discipline to mold us and develop us into the person he wants us to be.

You Travel Alone But God Is Always With You

We have to go through our wilderness experience alone, none of our friends or family members can really understand our experience what God is doing in our lives; only God knows and understands. But God is always there with us. God often removes distractions like our "toys" and support networks so we will focus more closely on our relationship with him.

God Often Makes Us Wait

God makes us wait in the desert to build our faith, trust, character and perseverance. Waiting for God to answer in no fun, but he frequently makes us wait for answers to prayer, for changes in our personal lives and for changes in our life situation. God often waits for people to give up, and then he rescues them.

Waiting teaches us to acknowledge that he is God and we are not. Waiting builds intimacy and dependence on God. It brings out our true motives, builds anticipation and develops patience.

Waiting teaches us to submit without grumbling and to take advantage of present opportunities, while we wait for our prayers to be answered. Waiting teaches us to trust in God, not our circumstances, feelings or our thoughts. Waiting transforms our character.

God is waiting for his perfect time to reveal you.

The Desert Often Follows the Mountaintop

A wilderness experience will often immediately follow a mountaintop experience. Just as the Holy Spirit led Jesus into the wilderness immediately following his baptism, sometimes, we'll find ourselves in our own desert, right after some major victory or accomplishment. Jesus' journey through his wilderness experience demonstrated the greatest possible transformation and God's great pleasure at his success.

It could be that God wants to keep us humble after our victory, or it could be that Satan doesn't want you to solidify your recent spiritual growth and development.

Potential Wilderness Outcomes

As a result of your desert experience, you may draw closer to God, having developed an intimate relationship with him in the desert. You may have spent time in God's Word, in prayer, in worship, and in deep communion with God, and as a result, you leave the desert having grown and matured in your Christian walk.

As you spent time getting to know God – as he really is, not as you may have been taught – you may find that you need to redefine some of your beliefs about God and how he relates to us. That's all part of the transition process as you assimilate what you've learned.

The wilderness experience is a time of testing, challenge and transformation; but God doesn't force us to make the right choice. He's given us free will, and consequently, we are free to make any choice we want. Consequently, some people, like the elder son, will harden their hearts and choose to reject God and go their own way. That is not God's preferred choice, but he does allow us the freedom to reject him as well as choose him.

Wilderness Benefits

As difficult as it may seem, there are a number of benefits that result from spending time in the wilderness, in God's "boot camp:"

1) God prepares you for future service.
2) God positions you for greater power.
3) You can experience deep communion with God.
4) You develop intimacy with God in the wilderness.
5) The wilderness builds faith, perseverance and character.
6) Your trust in God can increase.
7) Wilderness teaches us to focus on the goodness of God.
8) You experience God's grace and protection.
9) You experience spiritual growth.
10) Wilderness breeds humility.
11) Suffering proves the genuineness of your faith.
12) The wilderness can create secure attachment with God.
13) You can gain insight into the mind of God in the wilderness.
14) You can exercise free will in the desert.

15) The wilderness confirms that we are children of God.

16) You discover you true "self" in the desert.

17) The wilderness produces a hunger for God's Word.

18) The wilderness experience produces spiritual growth.

19) The wilderness produces peace (flow) by focusing our time, energy and attention on immediate survival needs.

Next Steps

As mentioned earlier, all believers will get an invitation to the wilderness at some point in their lives; so if you haven't already had yours, it's coming … soon.

Start preparing now for that period of disruptive change in your life by putting down deep roots in the Word of God. Get involved in your church or Bible Study group and start learning more about how God thinks and what he expects from each of us. His goal is to create spiritual growth, development and maturity in each one of us. He wants to remove the chaff from our lives and purify us so that we will be ready for our mansion in the sky.

Do everything you can to cooperate with God when he taps you on the shoulder. Remember, he has a plan for your life, a plan for good, so trust him to bring it about.

PS: Keep this book handy, you never know when you might need to refer to some of the transformation principles we've discussed.

Endnotes

1. McCall, Thomas S, *Palestine vs. Israel as the Name of the Holy Land.* Levitt Letter. https://www.levitt.com/essays/palestine..

2. Payne, Philip Barton, "Parables," in *Baker's Evangelical Dictionary of the Bible.* https://www.biblestudytools.com/dictionaries/bakers-evangelical-dictionary/parable.html.

3. Puskas, C. B., and Crump, D. *An Introduction to the Gospels and Acts.* (Grand Rapids, MI: William B. Eerdmans Publishing Company, 2008), Cambridge, U.K., 16.

4. Countryman, W, (1988), *Dirt, Sex and Greed.* (Philadelphia: Fortress Press, 1988), 150.

5. Edersheim, A, T*he Life and Times of Jesus the Messiah.* (McLean VA: Macdonald Publishing Co), 91-92.

6. Herford, p 68,69, as quoted in: https://bible.org/seriespage/zealots#P28_5794.

7. Hagner, *The Jewish Reclamation of Jesus,* 137-141.

8. *The Weightier Matters (Part I): Introduction.* https://www.bibletools.org/index.cfm/fuseaction/Topical.show/RTD/cgg/ID/1211/Pharisees.htm.

9. Payne, Philip Barton, "Parables," in *Baker's Evangelical Dictionary of the Bible.*

10. Edersheim, A., T*he Life and Times of Jesus the Messiah,* 580-595.

11. Tenney, M., *The Zondervan Pictorial Encyclopedia of the Bible,* Volume Four, M-P, 593.

12. Countryman, L. William, *Dirt, Greed, and Sex: Sexual Ethics in the New Testament and Their Implications for Today* (Kindle Location 3159). Kindle Edition.

13. *The New International Dictionary of New Testament of Theology.* Vol. One, A-F, ed. C. Brown (Grand Rapids, MI: Zondervan, 1971), 614-615.

14. Packer, J.I., *Knowing God,* (Downers Grove, IL, InterVarsity Press, 1973), 187-188.

15. Tenney, M, *The Zondervan Pictorial Encyclopedia of the Bible,* 61.

16. Countryman, *Dirt, Sex and Greed,* 188.

17. *The New International Dictionary of New Testament of Theology.* Vol. 2, ed. C. Brown (Grand Rapids, MI, 1976), Zondervan, 295.

18. Bailey, Kenneth E, *Jacob and the Prodigal: How Jesus Retold Israel's Story.* InterVarsity Press. Kindle Edition. P. 54.

19. Payne, Philip Barton, in *Baker's Evangelical Dictionary of the Bible, Parables.* https://www.biblestudytools.com/dictionaries/bakers-evangelical-dictionary/parable.html.

20. Bailey, Kenneth E, *Finding the Lost Cultural Keys to Luke 15* (Concordia Scholarship Today) (Kindle Locations 767-783), Concordia Publishing House. Kindle Edition.

21. Grant, Michael, *Jesus: An Historian's Review of the Gospels,* 1995, 10-11

22 http://www.swapmeetdave.com/Bible/Parables/index.htm, taken from: *NIV Narrated Bible in Chronological Order* (hardcover) and *Daily Bible in Chronological Order* (paperback) by Dr. F. LaGard Smith of Pepperdine University, published by Harvest House.

23 Payne, Philip Barton, "Parables," in *Baker's Evangelical Dictionary of the Bible*, https://www.biblestudytools.com/dictionaries/bakers-evangelical-dictionary/parable.html.

24 "The Parable of the Prodigal Son," in *Journey of a Lifelong Disciple*, https://journeyofalifelongdisciple.wordpress.com/2013/06/08/the-parable-of-the-prodigal-son/.

25 Anderson, R, *On Being Human: Essays on Theological Anthropology,* 16

26 Schreck, G, *"Personhood and Relational Life Tasks," in* H. Vande Kamp ed. *Family Therapy: Christian Perspective,* (Grand Rapids, MI, 1991), Baker Book House, 50.

27 Anderson, R, *On Being Human: Essays on Theological Anthropology,* (Pasadena, CA: Fuller Theological Seminary Press, 1982), 177.

28 Taylor, B.B., "Four Stops in the Wilderness," *Journal for Preachers* 24/2 (2001), 5.

29 Packer, J.I., *Knowing God,* (Downers Grove, IL, InterVarsity Press, 1973), 35-37.

30 Schreck, P, in *Family Therapy: Christian Perspectives,* (Grand Rapids, MI: Baker Book House, 1991), ed. H. Vande Kamp, 95.

31 Brown, Volume I, 642.

32 28 *Matthew Henry's Bible Commentary (concise).* https://www.christianity.com/bible/commentary.php?com=mhc&b=21&c=11, retrieved 11/4/18.

33 Bailey, Kenneth E, *Finding the Lost Cultural Keys to Luke 15,* (Kindle Locations 2015-4000).

34 Bailey, Kenneth E, *Jacob and the Prodigal: How Jesus Retold Israel's Story,* 105.

35 Nouwen, H., *The Return of the Prodigal Son: A Meditation on Fathers, Brothers, and Sons,* (New York: Doubleday, 1992), 114.

36 Nouwen, H., *The Return of the Prodigal Son: A Meditation on Fathers, Brothers, and Sons,* 119. (bold, mine).

37 Nouwen, H., *The Return of the Prodigal Son: A Meditation on Fathers, Brothers, and Sons,* 114.

38 Schreck, P, in *Family Therapy: Christian Perspectives,* 90.

39 Packer, J.I., *Knowing God,* (Downers Grove, IL, InterVarsity Press, 1973), 185.

40 Schreck, P, in *Family Therapy: Christian Perspectives,,* 95.

41 Nouwen, H., *The Return of the Prodigal Son: A Meditation on Fathers, Brothers, and Sons,* 4.

42 Friedman, M., *The Healing Dialogue in Psychotherapy,* (Northvale, NJ: Jason Aronson), 28-29.

43 Packer, J.I., *Knowing God,* (Downers Grove, IL, 1973), 185.

44 Nouwen, H., *The Return of the Prodigal Son: A Meditation on Fathers, Brothers, and Sons,* 123.

45 *"The Parable of the Prodigal Son,"* in *Journey of a Lifelong Disciple.* https://journeyofalifelongdisciple.wordpress.com/2013/06/08/the-parable-of-the-prodigal-son/.

46 "Luke 15 Bible Commentary," in *John Gill's Exposition of the Bible.* https://www.christianity.com/bible/commentary.php?com=gill&b=42&c=15.

47 "The Parable of the Prodigal Son," in *Journey of a Lifelong Disciple.* https://journeyofalifelongdisciple.wordpress.com/2013/06/08/the-parable-of-the-prodigal-son/.

48 Nouwen, H., *The Return of the Prodigal Son: A Meditation on Fathers, Brothers, and Sons,* 35.

Made in the USA
Lexington, KY
28 March 2019